Second Chances

Moonlight Mile Ranch Series: Book 1

Mel Sobolewski

Second Chances

This is a work of fiction. Any resemblance to actual persons, living or dead, is purely coincidental.

ISBN: 9798987129692

Library of Congress Control Number: 2023938096

Cover Design and Art by Chad Pinckney

Cover Photo by Willie Toledo

Published in 2023 by All Things that Matter Press

To Veronica, my still, always, and forever.

CHAPTER ~ 1

Hickory

Sagebrush Farm was nestled between two mountain ranges in Malibu, California. Shortly after his wife passed away, Slick purchased the land, thinking it would be a new beginning for him and his daughter June. The property was large, about ten acres, covered in trees, grass, and rolling hills. With some work, Slick knew that he could transform the land into something special, and he would finally be able to rescue a horse he promised June.

Over the years, Sagebrush Farm became more than just a home to June's horse. It became home to many horses whose owners paid board each month. Slick and June would host fundraisers, bingo nights, and private dinners twice a month. They would open the farm to their community for all to enjoy a day in nature and learning about horse care.

One of the horses that lived on this property was Hickory. He resided in Pasture Three with his friend Boomer. Boomer was June's horse. Hickory spent his days napping under the oak tree, eating his bucket of grain, and, a few times a month, would take a trail ride with Boomer, Slick, and June. Hickory spent his nights munching on hay, star-gazing, and listening to all the nocturnal animals sing.

One afternoon in the Santa Monica Mountains, a power outage occurred in a power company line. The spark snapped the electrical lines, and when the wire landed on the ground, it started a brush fire. Unfortunately, brush fires are common in California because of its dry climate, frequent droughts, and abundant forest fuels like dried and dead branches and leaves.

Firefighters can prevent brush fires from spreading, but this was no ordinary fire. This fire happened on a day when fire warnings were high as it was dry and windy. The Santa Ana winds, also known as the "devil's wind" are infamous for spreading wildfires, were so extreme that the fire grew big and fast. Fire departments from all over southern California tried to put the fire out, but it was unstoppable. For two days, this fire burned, jumping highways and demolished historic western movie sets. It touched the Pacific coastline and ultimately destroyed several cities before being contained.

***

Slick was no stranger to fire season. He knew his farm was in danger as they were only a few miles from where the wire came down. "Hey, June," Slick shouted. "We must get the horses out of here before the fire comes our way. The winds are powerful, and it's going to move fast. I don't know in what direction, but it is always better for us to be safe and take precautions. We should start by loading the horses that have a hard time getting into the trailer. Boomer and Hickory will go last as they are comfortable in trailers. I'll drive the first group down the mountain and return to get you."

June immediately agreed to the plan, and they got to work. As Slick drove down the mountain with a trailer of horses, he looked out into the distance and saw what he feared. Thick clouds of smoke and flames were heading their way. He began to wonder if that was the last time he would see Sagebrush Farm. He was concerned about June and the two boys but he knew they would find a way out. Their family had been practicing fire evacuations for years.

At the foothill, Slick met neighbors who were also evacuating their farm animals. There were goats, sheep, donkeys, ponies, dogs, and more, covered with soot, desperately drinking clean cold fresh water out of large portable water bins in a parking lot across the street from a gas station and Del Taco. Veterinary technicians tended to incisions and burns some horses incurred on the trailer ride down the mountain. Trailers are made of metal, so they can heat up quickly when the fire is close.

"My goodness," were the first words Slick muttered to the volunteers that came over to help him. "Thank you all for being here and helping me unload my horses. I need everyone to be careful. They are anxious and nervous. I don't want any horses or humans to get hurt as they exit the trailer. I have to go back up the mountain! My daughter and two more horses are waiting for me." Slick got back into his truck and began driving up the mountain when a fireman stopped him.

"Nope. We're not letting anyone up this road. The only vehicles allowed are firetrucks. We can't risk any injuries or accidents that could prevent us from doing our jobs," said the fireman.

"But listen, my farm is a short way up the road. My daughter and two horses are waiting for me to help them evacuate. You gotta let me go through," Slick said anxiously.

"I can't allow anyone to go up this road. The fire is still burning strong," the fireman responded.

Slick felt his heart beat faster, knowing the incredible danger that June and the horses faced. He tried to text June, but there was no cell service as all power was cut off, and the lines were full of people trying to connect with loved ones. Slick then parked his trailer and walked back to his horses. He put one hand on Rudy's back and the other over his heart and began taking deep breaths. After several minutes, Slick knew that June would get the horses and herself out safely. Slick thanked Rudy, a beautiful Palomino horse belonging to one of the boarders, for helping him stay grounded and focused on the tasks that faced him. After that, Slick started to help all the animals that came off the mountain with injuries.

***

June waited for her father to arrive at the barn but began to wonder if something wasn't right. Round trips down the mountain never took more than fifteen minutes, and the only vehicles on the road were firetrucks driving at top speed. She thought, *Dad should have been back by now. The fire must be close, and road barricades will not let him back up the mountain. I haven't seen a civilian car in a while. Just firetrucks with firemen shouting to evacuate now! It's time to set the boys free."*

June put on her helmet, jumped on her dirt bike, kickstarted the engine, and sped down the road to Pasture Three. The winds were picking up, making the bike hard to steer. Smoke tornados were forming all around, blowing dirt and debris in her path. When she looked back, she saw flames starting to touch the far side of the property where their barn was located. When June made visual contact with Hickory and Boomer, they were neighing loudly, rearing and pacing anxiously along the perimeter of their pasture.

June tried to open the lock to their pasture, but the metal was too hot to touch. She put on her gloves, unlocked the gate, and stood calmly in their pasture to help ease their worry. Fortunately, she was able to get the two focused long enough to slide their halters over their necks and used a Sharpie marker to write their names and her dad's phone number. June attached lead ropes to their halters and walked the boys out of the pasture, "Listen to me. I am leading you away from the fire, trusting that your instincts will carry you along in that direction. Do not head back to the barn or the farm. It is no longer a safe place. You boys will need to look out for each other and stay together. Dad and I will send a rescue team to find you. The information on your halters will let them know you are part of our family. Your job is to get to safety. I love you both. Now go!" June unclipped their lead ropes, set them free, and watched the horses run until they were out of her sight.

***

June grew up with animals and believed in the power of animal communication. She knew that Hickory and Boomer understood what she was saying by the way they looked directly into her eyes. While she spoke, the horses tried to focus on June despite the chaos surrounding them. Now that Hickory and Boomer were running free and all the other horses were safe, it was time for June to leave too and find her dad.

She got back on her bike and rode out of the property. From the main road, she watched the fire ravage the brown barn, burning all the horses' name plates that she painted to match their personalities. She witnessed her favorite tree that she loved to read under catch fire. The hay shed she set up with her dad was gone too. Everything June and Slick created over the years was ruined in minutes. As destruction fell upon the Sagebrush Farm, she thought about a mythical story she once read under her favorite tree about a Phoenix that rose from ashes. It was a story of renewal. And in that moment, she knew that she and her father would rebuild as they did before.

***

Hickory and Boomer galloped up the mountains, across a dried-out creek, through a burning vineyard, and eventually, made it to the end of a familiar trail. That night, they slept close to each other to feel safe. They woke at sunrise, confused. The air was still thick with smoke. There was no water or breakfast. They were scared, but they had each other, which was enough to keep them going.

***

Slick called an animal search and rescue team he knew to help locate Hickory and Boomer. "Hey, Lori, are you involved in rescuing animals in the Woolsey Fire?"

"Slick. It is so good to hear from you. I am doing animal rescues. What's up?" Lori replied.

"June had to set two of our horses free as we couldn't evacuate them in time. My gut tells me they are somewhere near Butte Trail; we ride there a few times a month. I can share the location of the trailhead and a photo of the horses. Their halters are marked with their names and my cell number. The fire department is not letting me anywhere near the farm. No access is allowed, so I can't go looking for them. I need your help finding them," Slick said.

"I just received the information you sent. My team is working with the fire department, so I can access all roads that would otherwise be blocked off to the public. I'll get looking for them immediately," Lori said and hung up the phone.

***

Lori was exhausted from walking the trail and searching for the horses but knew she couldn't return without them. As she finally reached the overlook at the top of Butte Trail, she noticed movement ahead. "Hickory! Boomer," she yelled and heard a raspy neigh and moved faster. There they were, standing side by side, looking directly at her. One was a large, beautiful grey, white Andalusian horse whose halter read Boomer. And the other was a handsome brown Rocky Mountain horse whose halter read Hickory. Lori inspected their bodies for injuries. They had cuts all over their legs from galloping through the hills. Their hair was charred from the fire. Their noses were swollen from breathing in the smoke. None of these injuries would prevent the horses from getting off the mountain. Lori gave them some water, attached a lead rope to their halters, and guided them to the trailer parked on the side of the road. As Lori navigated her way down, she began to think about their endurance and bravery escaping such a destructive fire.

The other animals Lori had been rescuing were not set free and remained on the owner's properties and barns. This rescue was different as it showed the resilience and power of a horse. She reassured them, "Slick and June will be so happy that you are okay. I'll call Slick once we are safe to let him know where to meet us. You boys are going to a shelter where other animals rescued from the fire are being treated. You'll be fed and have plenty of water and clean air. We will get you both cleaned up."

***

Slick and June arrived at the shelter just as Lori unloaded the boys. They gave Hickory and Boomer big hugs and walked them into their new stalls. "Lori, I can't thank you enough for your help. We lost everything. Our house and barn are gone," Slick said.

"I'm so sorry to hear that," Lori responded.

"We got all the boarded horses out alive, and June set our two horses free just as the fire began to burn our property down. The horses are what mattered most. The owners of the boarded horses have independently made new living arrangements throughout California, which is wonderful news. But without a home or barn, June and I cannot care for Boomer and Hickory. We need to put them up for adoption. My time and money will be spent finding temporary housing. Mentally, that is about as far as I can plan right now. Boomer is our most recent adoption. We got him from a shelter in Palm Springs. He was running free in the desert until animal control picked him up. Hickory's story is more complex. His owner, Ray, stopped paying board. The rules at our farm are that if an owner doesn't pay the board for several months, we can claim possession of the horse. Heck, I can't even remember the last time I saw or heard from Ray. At one point, Ray was spending every day with Hickory. Then it all just stopped. Nothing happened to Ray. He's still living in Malibu someplace. He just quit on the guy, even without saying goodbye. As time passed, Hickory felt the absence of Ray, and his personality changed. He was sad, confused, and heartbroken. He walked slower, hung his head low, and rarely made eye contact. Hickory trusted him. That trust was broken. So, I put Boomer into his pasture, thinking that would lift his spirits. They became friends; it was a mentorship relationship. June and I were devastated, so we took him in as our own. I gave him extra love and included him on our trail rides. I thought getting him out working, breathing, and walking would be good. This decision to put them up for adoption doesn't come easy or without weighing all options. We've put years into knowing these horses. I know we both care deeply for these boys," Slick said.

"Yeah, Boomer and I were really starting to bond. But I know the level of care that these horses need and deserve. I'm working hard to accept this decision, as they are part of our family, even though it's the right one," June said while kissing Hickory on the nose.

"June, you're brave and very wise. No wonder they trusted you during the fire. Hickory and Boomer are remarkable horses. Their new owners will be lucky to have them! I know I'd be so happy with a horse like Boomer. Rest assured that they will be taken care of and receive lots of loving attention while they're here," Lori said as she scratched Boomer's belly.

"Interesting you say that. We were wondering if you'd be open to adopting Boomer. I want to give him to you as a thank you for finding our boys. Do you still have the stall in your backyard? Boomer is young and healthy. You already know how wonderful he is. I think you would enjoy working with him, and he'd enjoy being trained by you. My intuition tells me you two are a good fit," Slick said.

"Are you serious! Yes. I have enough land for another horse to be added to our herd. I'd be honored to be Boomer's new mom. I love training young horses. Thank you so much, Slick." Lori joyfully replied and kissed Boomer's nose.

"Lori, maybe I can visit him sometime? I want him to know that this decision comes from a place of love, not abandonment." June said.

"June, anytime you want to see Boomer, you are welcome. I grew up with horses. These bonds are unbreakable. They become part of you," Lori said.

"Now, Hickory is older. I know that senior horses are harder to adopt. I don't want him to end up in the wrong home. He can't jump from owner to owner. That never ends well. He doesn't deserve that kind of treatment. Hickory is kind; you can see it in his eyes. Even right now. After surviving such a traumatic event, he shows you his gentle soul. He listens and, most of all, he loves. He doesn't need to be worked like Boomer, who is young and full of energy. Hickory needs trusted companionship more than anything else. A family that he can rely on. He's already been through so much: Ray's abandonment and then the fire. I'm gutted over this decision." Slick began crying.

"My dad and I always talk about the lifespan of a horse and how they can live to be thirty years old. And then we think about how many homes a horse can have within that time. Especially as they age and can no longer work like a young horse. That is when they are at the most risk to be shuffled around from home to home.

One of the most magical things about Hickory is his wisdom and strength that comes with age and life experience. His friendship is the best of all," June said.

"June, that is very true. When I adopt a horse, I keep them for their life. So don't you ever worry about Boomer. Experiencing the growth and change within the relationship is very profound. I promise to find a good home for Hickory. I took a full-time job at this shelter to have access to the animals. I'll watch over him and the adoption process," Lori said as she hugged Slick and June.

***

That very same day, Mel, who was also rescuing animals from the fire, brought her daughter Lennon, and Mojo, Lennon's big dog brother, to the shelter where Hickory was recovering. Mel was checking on all the animals she rescued. The three of them began to feed the rescued ducks, pigs, cows, donkeys, goats, and bunnies. As they made their way to the horses, Lennon and Mojo ran ahead to meet the new one. Hickory greeted them by nodding his head. When Mel caught up, she greeted Hickory too and began scratching his forehead. Hickory leaned into the scratches and nickered.

"Excuse me, do you happen to know the name of this horse?" Mel asked Lori while pointing to Hickory.

Lori was in the next stall, grooming Boomer, and told them the story of Hickory's heroic escape from the fire. In the end, she purposely let them know that Hickory was up for adoption.

Mel and Lennon stood there, looking at Lori and Hickory in amazement. And before Mel could say a word, Hickory opened his mouth and took her cowboy hat right off her head! As he played with it, Lennon began belly-laughing. Mojo was jumping around like a bunny and barking with excitement. Admiring the joy surrounding them, Mel started thinking about the responsibilities of adopting a horse. Through animal rescue, she developed a network of people she could trust to help her learn more about horsemanship. She knew she could provide for the horse in terms of medical care and food. And while Mel went back and forth in her head, making logical points, her heart had already decided to adopt Hickory.

As Hickory ate carrots from Lennon's hand, Mel noticed kindness in his eyes but also a hint of sadness, fear, and longing to be loved. Mel knew she'd never understand what Hickory experienced during the fire but knew he needed to be with a safe and loving family.

"Lennon, would you like Hickory to be part of our family? He can be your older horse brother," Mel said

"Yes, I do! Brother Hickory, here you go," Lennon said as she handed him another carrot.

"But listen, Lennon, when we adopt an animal, we're committing to take care of the animal for the rest of his or her life. This is more than just a financial commitment. It's spending time with him and caring for him just as we care for ourselves. Hickory is 19 years old and can live to be 30 years old or older. Are you sure?" Mel asked.

"Yes, I am, Mom! And as a family, we stick together. We will love him forever," Lennon said as she put her hands on her mother's cheeks.

"I know we will," Mel responded and kissed Lennon on her head.

The adoption papers were signed, and Hickory had a new family.

***

Mel spent her entire adulthood living in the city of Los Angeles and recently purchased a plot of land for space and nature. The property was a real work in progress as the only structure in place was a small house. Mel imagined the property would ultimately be a fantastic location for Hickory, but nothing was set up to care for horses.

"Lori, listen, I have a piece of land. I think I can transform it into a wonderful home for Hickory. But I need help. I don't know much about horses or how to build a barn. Do you know anyone that can help? And do you know anyone that can help me care for Hickory while fences are being put up?" Mel asked.

"Well, if this isn't the most serendipitous moment I have ever witnessed, then I don't know what is. I'm going to give you a number; his name is Slick. He built his barn, his pastures, an arena, and more. He knows a ton about land development and animal care. He lost everything in the fire. Hickory, your horse, lived at his boarding facility. He just put Hickory up for adoption moments before you came here. Boomer was also one of his horses. But now this handsome fella is mine. Call Slick. In the meantime, there's a private home in Ojai where you can keep Hickory until your property is ready. I have boarded my horses at this ranch. It's a great transition for everyone," Lori said, smiling.

"Wow, these are a lot of interesting connections. It's meant to be," Mel said to Lori and walked to a quiet area with Lennon and Mojo to call Slick.

"Hi, Slick. My name is Mel. Lori gave me your number," Mel said.

"Oh, hi. How can I help you?" Slick answered.

"Well, my family and I just adopted Hickory, and we are very excited about it. I own some land about thirty minutes from the shelter. I don't have anything in place to home a horse. I was wondering if you could help? I'd pay for the services," Mel said.

"Well, this is wild. I'm happy Hickory found himself a good home. I would love to help, but my daughter and I don't even have a place to live. I need to figure out our next steps before taking on a new project. I'm sorry about that," Slick answered, defeated.

"Listen, Slick. This fire was a life-changing event for everyone that crossed its path. It changed me. You. Hickory. I'm trusting the universe here, and I think Hickory connected us for a reason. You don't have a place to live. I need to build Hickory a home. Why don't we get an Airstream and park it on my property? You and June can live there. I'll hire you to help me build out my land for Hickory and maybe a few other horses down the line," Mel suggested.

"I'm not sure what to say. This is the nicest offer I have ever received. I'm humbled and taken back. We did lose everything. We have no income. It's just us and the clothes on our backs. I can't say no to this offer. Yes. Absolutely." Slick wiped his tearing eyes.

"Fantastic. We can talk more about this over lunch tomorrow. Bring your daughter. She can meet Lennon," Mel said.

Arrangements were made, and it was time for Hickory to leave the shelter and be transferred to his temporary housing in Ojai. When the trailer pulled into the ranch, there were two massive green pastures. One was an old baseball field converted into a cow pasture. The pasture adjacent was filled with llamas and alpacas that watched the trailer, anxiously waiting to see who was inside. When Mojo jumped out of Mel's pick-up truck, the llamas weren't disappointed and followed his every movement. Mostly, they watched Mojo pee on every tree in their sight. The barn where Hickory was going to stay was once used for the cows that now freely roamed the old baseball field, so the stalls were massive. The owner of the property kept her horses in the same barn. All the horses were spoiled. Hickory had new acquaintances to keep him company. Each stall faced rolling green mountains covered in yellow and purple flowers. There were bunnies burrowing in the hay, and chipmunks bravely surfaced from their underground tunnels searching for food. The goats were in the hills, grazing on the brush and invasive flowers that could be a potential fire risk. Occasionally, a cow would stroll over to drink out of Hickory's water tank. Hickory settled in.

Lennon, Mojo, and Mel visited several times a week. Lennon loved to run around the barn, watching her mom complete the chores, such as mucking the stable and picking dirt and rocks out of Hickory's hooves. On scorching days, Lennon would hose Hickory down with water. She loved putting her hand into his water tank to try and touch the fish working hard to keep his water clean of algae. Mojo chased bunnies, stared at the alpacas while they stared back at him, rolled in horse poop, and took naps in the shade. Lennon climbed the piles of hay, jumping to the ground, shouting, "Hickory" over and over. Hickory would nicker and watch her. They brought watermelon, and the three of them enjoyed eating it together. Hickory was the messiest of eaters. He drooled watermelon juice all over Lennon's head and clothes. Lennon, Mojo, and Mel celebrated Christmas and New Year's Day with Hickory, and when the family came in from out of town, a visit to Hickory was their first stop.

The more time Mel spent with Hickory, the more they began to trust each other. Mel talked to him about her experiences in the fire. While grooming him, she explained the tight feeling in her lungs from inhaling all the smoke as she drove around Malibu, searching for animals. She asked Hickory if he remembered that familiar feeling. Like most horses at the shelter, Hickory had severe inflammation in his nasal canals from all the smoke. While mucking his stall, Mel told Hickory about her rescue where she found a family's chickens by following dropped eggs in the backyard that led her from their empty chicken coop into the family's den, where all the chickens were running around. The family brought them into their house, thinking they'd be safer. And one of the most uplifting stories she shared with Hickory was about a woman who flooded her entire home by turning on all the faucets and showers and leaving the doors open to her yard in order to save her tortoise, Otis. She was forced to evacuate quickly, and the smoke filled her home making it impossible for her to find him in time. Tortoises are smart and part of the reason they survived this long is their ability to escape danger by burying themselves deep into the ground. Otis survived and a team of rescuers found him several feet below the surface in the woman's backyard not far from the door she kept open. It was essential to Mel that Hickory knew of the human bravery that took place during the fire. It was a bunch of fearless locals that came together to save as many animals as possible.

As Hickory began to feel secure, he showed gratitude for his new family. When he napped, he put his head in Mel's lap and let her stroke his face softly and slowly. When Lennon entered Hickory's pasture, he bowed his head down to her height so she could kiss his nose. When Mel gave Hickory his grain bowl full of additional nutrients, Hickory shared his bowl with Mojo, no matter how much he loved his coconut-flavored pellets. Hickory was gentle, loving, and playful. When it was time to say goodnight, Lennon whispered to him that he would be forever loved, protected, and part of their family. Sometimes, when she sensed that he was anxious, releasing his past traumas, she'd leave him her favorite lovey bear that made her feel calm and to help him at night.

During this time, Slick worked hard to get the land set up. The pasture fencing was complete, using a weathered natural brown wood. The barn matched the fencing and stood tall and proud. There was a small arena for Hickory to run in and a washing post for baths. The feed shed was complete, and a fresh order of hay was waiting for Hickory.

"Well, Mel. The property is ready. It's time to bring Hickory home. We did this together. I am so grateful to you for helping June and me. I didn't know my next steps, and like an angel, you came in and offered me a job and housing. Thank you for trusting us," Slick said.

"Slick. If I have learned anything in this life, it is that we need to be kind and compassionate to each other. Connection is why we are all here. I am forever grateful to you, too, for helping me transform a plot of land into a beautiful home for Hickory. There is gratitude both ways," Mel said.

"I'm really excited to see Hickory. I can't wait to hug him," June said.

"June, you set him free and saved his life," Mel said.

"When I was riding off the property. I had this vision of the Phoenix rising. Do you know that story?" June asked.

"Sure do," Mel answered.

"Anyway, the vision that came to me was my dad and I rebuilding Sagebrush. But that wasn't our path. It was to meet your family and build something new together. I can tell already that this is going to be an awesome place. A place we can call home, too," June said.

"I think so, June," Slick said. "Now, Mel, you got a horse in Ojai, waiting for you to pick him up and bring him home," Slick said and tossed her the truck keys.

"We sure do. Lennon, Mojo, in the truck, let's go get our boy," Mel said and began to pull the truck and trailer out of the property.

"Mel, you gotta name this place! You can't have a barn without a name. Think about it on your drive," Slick shouted.

The drive to Ojai went fast. When they arrived, Hickory knew they were coming to get him and was waiting by the stall door. Mojo walked over to the llamas and alpacas, and, for the first time ever, he let them sniff his tail. Then he ran back to the barn. Lennon got Hickory's halter and lead rope and handed them to Mel.

"I sure am going to miss those cows. So I'll go say goodbye," Lennon said.

Mel got Hickory into the trailer without any issue. The trailer window was open, and Hickory stuck his head out, , took one last look around and then began eating hay waiting for his family.

"Hey, Len, we are all ready. Are you?" Mel asked.

"Sure am," Lennon ran back to the truck and got in. Mojo jumped in after her.

"Slick said we need a barn name. I never really thought about one. But then again, I never had a barn before," Mel said and turned on the radio.

"Can we name the barn anything?" Lennon asked.

"Well, it should have some meaning. To us, to Hickory," Mel answered.

The radio played low, but the first few chords were recognizable to Mel.

"Lennon, this is the Rolling Stones. I love this song, *Moonlight Mile*," Mel said,

"Turn it louder. What is the song about?" Lennon asked.

"Well, the song is about coming home. The Rolling Stones traveled the world, playing their music to crowds of people, but nothing was as sweet and familiar as the road home," Mel said.

"How about that? Moonlight Mile Ranch. That is what we should name our barn. We are bringing Hickory home," Lennon asked.

"We are bringing him home. I love it!" Mel smiled.

When they pulled onto the property, June and Slick were there, waiting.

Mel got out of the truck, walked back, and opened the trailer doors. She took Hickory's lead rope and walked him out. When he had all four hooves on the dirt road, he let out a beautiful, loud neigh.

Hickory walked up to June and put his head down. She began to pet his forehead and then hugged him. Hickory looked at Slick and walked over to him next. Slick scratched his withers like he used to and gave him a tremendous hug. "It is sure good to see you, old friend," Slick said to Hickory.

Mel, Lennon, Slick, June, and Mojo walked Hickory down a dirt road to his new pasture where his favorite hay and grain bowl was waiting. Hickory is a story of love and a love for a special horse that brought the most unusual people together. And while Hickory was the first horse at Moonlight Mile Ranch, he sure wouldn't be the last.

CHAPTER ~2~

A Pig Named Love

Mel, Lennon, and Mojo were taking a family vacation in Big Bear, California when Mel received a call from an unknown number in Nebraska. The voice on the other end sounded anxious. "Hello. Is this Mel? My name is Frank. I own a feed store just outside of Omaha. I received your number from an animal welfare organization and followed your rescues during the Woolsey Fire. I have family that lives in Southern California. A bomb cyclone hit

Nebraska the other day. This means heavy rain and rapid snow melt have caused catastrophic flooding across the Mississippi River Basin. Rivers have been overflowing, putting most of the state underwater. The flooding destroyed bridges, roads, and homes and made small islands accessible only by a small motor or rowboats. All kinds of animals are stranded on these islands without food and water. We have tried to lead the horses and cows to higher ground, but getting them to cross the water is impossible."

"I have a horse, and he has a hard time crossing water as he cannot see the ground. So anything uncertain, he stays away from. So what are the farmers responsible for these animals doing?" Mel asked.

"Some of them are trying to help. Others have food and labor shortages.   And some are not doing anything but collecting money."

"What do you mean?" asked Mel.

"Well, if their animals pass away in a natural disaster, the farmers will receive insurance money. It's business. So, can you come out and help?" Frank asked.

"I am going to get some more information. First, I need to make sure that I can assemble the right team. Rescuing alone is impossible," Mel responded.

Mel and Lennon were very upset about the call, and they knew they needed to find out as much as possible about the flooding in Nebraska and its effect on the animals. But unfortunately, nothing about the floods was being reported on any major news networks. So Mel called her friends at Midwest Animal Search and Rescue, an animal rescue organization, to find out if they had any details on the flooding. Sarah, one of the owners, answered her call.

"It's true. The weather is dangerous all over Nebraska. It's a complicated situation as some people want help and others don't. If you are comfortable with potentially leaving with zero animals rescued, then let's go, girl! Our team will meet you," Sarah said.

"Are there other rescue teams in the field?" Mel asked.

"None that I am aware of. But that doesn't mean there aren't individual efforts," Sarah said.

"We need to try. Some people are asking for help directly," Mel said.

When they hung up the phone, Mel booked plane tickets for herself, Lennon, and Mojo and began to pack and plan. Mojo was a registered service dog, so he was able to fly on the plane with Mel and Lennon. Mel then called Slick to confirm that he'd feed Hickory while they were out of town. He was happy to help in any way he could.

When they landed in Omaha, Mel received a voicemail from Abigail at Country Road Animal Rescue. Country Road Animal Rescue was an animal sanctuary based in Colorado. Abigail, the owner, stated, "any cow, goat, pig rescued should be driven to Country Road where the animal will have land to roam, food to eat, and plenty of love for the remainder of their lives."

Mel returned Abigail's call. "Abigail, thank you so much for offering your rescue to the animals. We have a list of places to visit. I'll keep you posted, and yes, any animal rescued will live at Country Road. Thank you."

Their first stop was Frank's Feed Store. "Hey, Mel, it is so good to meet and see you. Thank you for coming. Now listen, my feed store provides food for the surrounding four counties. There are over 15,000 animals out there. We can't feed any of them. Our hay supply was ruined in the rain. Each new shipment heading our way gets diverted to other towns. Our animals are hungry. Can you get us hay? We will be in charge of its distribution. We have small boats lined up and extra hands to get to the animals stranded on islands," Frank asked.

Lennon looked up at Frank. "I'm Lennon. Our horse Hickory can share his hay!" And just then, Mel realized that Slick could place an order with Moonlight Mile's hay distributor located in

Texas. Texas was far enough away where there wouldn't be a supply issue. Most of the hay coming into Nebraska to help came from Iowa and Illinois.

Mel called Slick. "We're in Nebraska, trying to help the animals in this bomb cyclone. Is there any way you can direct a shipment of two semi-trucks of hay to a feed store out here?"

"Mel, be careful out there. Stay on the line while I make the call," Slick replied. He put them on hold for a few minutes and came back on. "Not a problem. Put me in touch with Frank, and I'll coordinate the delivery. Two trucks will be leaving Texas tonight and will arrive at the feed store in two days."

Frank looked relieved. "Oh, man! I am grateful. I could cry. I am cryin'. A grown man, cryin'. How about that. Now that I have confirmation of a hay delivery, I'll see if I can borrow some feed from another county till our shipment arrives. We'll then replace what we borrowed. Lennon, you sure are smart. Stick around here; we could use a bright mind like yours."

"Frank. We need to save the animals now. Feed the horses. Tell them Lennon says hi." Lennon turned around and walked out of the store. Mojo followed.

While they were with Frank, Mel received several text messages about a flooded farm where pigs were raised for food. Mel knew this would be an intense job and called Midwest Animal Search and Rescue. They agreed to meet there.

As Mel drove to the next spot, which was only thirty minutes down the highway, she warned Lennon about what they could possibly see.

"Lennon, we're on our way to a pig farm. The pigs you are about to see will be much bigger than the potbelly pigs you have seen in the past. These pigs can grow to be 800 pounds. They are raised for food and will not be trusting of humans. Remember, how we treat animals directly impacts who they become. Exactly like us. Our life experiences shape our personalities and views of the world. Animals not treated well will not feel safe around people. Even the ones trying to help," Mel said.

"Why would a human hurt an animal?" Lennon questioned.

"That is a hard question, and I don't know the answer. Animals are considered property and a food source for humans. Because they're property, humans can treat animals however they want with little repercussion. Being an animal rescuer or advocate is hard work as we fight for equality and justice for all living animals. These are not easy principles to change, as information about what is a nutritional diet and cultural traditions have been engrained in us for generations. While we can't force, we can live by setting an example and inspiring others to be kinder to all.

"Sharing our animal rescue stories is a great place to start. Listen, the most impactful change happens one decision at a time," Mel answered.

"Equality, like in the books we read at school. Is this a mean farm?" Lennon questioned.

"Mean is hard to define as people can see the same situation differently. In our eyes, yes. We believe that all animals can feel. That they are sentient beings. We believe that all living species are equal and should be treated respectfully. We believe they are not here for us to use as we please. But sadly, not everyone thinks as we do. It is important to understand that people have different value systems," Mel responded.

"Why wouldn't they think like us?" Lennon asked.

"That is not the way the world works. Farming is a business, and how many companies make money. The farm we are driving to is called an agricultural farm. They are raising these pigs for bacon, pork, and other animal products," Mel replied.

"I'm sad. They will need love. All you need is love, love," Lennon began to sing.

"It is good to acknowledge your feelings of sadness and be with that feeling. I'm sad too. But listen, if we save one animal out of the hundreds that could be injured, we will have done a great job," Mel said.

Lennon responded, "Okay."

"All we can do is our best and be happy with that," Mel said. She then turned to Mojo. "Do not eat anything on the ground. Nothing, Mojo!" Mojo licked Mel's face and stuck his head out the window. Mojo was notorious for eating and rolling in other animals' poop on every farm he visited.

They turned off the highway and onto a long, narrow, muddy road. As Mel drove, the van's wheels kept sliding from left to right and getting stuck in the mud. The flooding caused ponds everywhere. They knew they were at the right property when Lennon spotted four large black and white pigs crossing the road in front of the van. At the end of the road was Midwest Animal Search and Rescue's trailer.

Walker, another owner of Midwest Animal Search and Rescue, walked around the property and came to their group for an update. "The conditions on this farm are much worse than I expected. Shelters have fallen, trapping pigs. Several of them have died. Many more are injured and are limping around. Some found a way to escape and made their way off the property. Let them walk free, or at least encourage them to continue. The mud is really thick, deep, and full of toxins. We will need mud boots and waterproof clothing. Luckily, we brought all that with us. Walking will be exhausting as our feet will sink deep. Drink some water now, and let's get ready as this rescue will take longer than we expected."

As Sarah was tying her boots, she leaned down. "Lennon and Mojo, it is so great to finally meet you. Mel has told me so much about your rescues and love for the animals. I think you two should stay in our truck while we are on the farm. It is safe and warm here. One of our team members, Natalie, will stand outside to watch the trailer. You can help us spot pigs that are injured. All you have to do is shout out the window to one of us. We'll hear you." Mojo jumped into their truck, and Sarah lifted Lennon and put her in the front seat.

"You got it," Lennon responded while pretending to turn the steering wheel.

As they began to put on their mud boots, bodysuits, and gloves, the farm owner came running over. "Wait right there! What are you doing here? I didn't call for any help," he yelled.

"Sir, we are here to help rescue some of these pigs. At first glance, many need a vet immediately," Walker responded calmly.

"They're not hurt! These are my animals. I know what's best for them. Now, leave us alone," the farmer responded angrily.

"We understand that you are upset. The storm that came through caused a ton of damage. We can see your property was hit really hard. We know this is stressful. It's okay to not be fine and allow us to help you," Mel said.

As they pleaded with him, a police officer walked down the road. "I was called here by one of your neighbors. They're concerned and said your pigs were running onto their property, looking for food, and some appeared hurt. These folks are here to help. I insist you let them. I will stick around here to ensure there is no trouble."

The farmer was still angry. "My neighbors wouldn't call the police on me. But since you are here, I will let you take one pig off my farm." After several minutes of negotiations and explaining that several needed medical attention, they agreed that the pig in the worst condition would be rescued.

Their team began searching for the pig needing the most medical attention. As they walked through each shelter, their feet sank deep into the mud, making walking difficult. They had to lift debris, cut through metal fencing and climb over heavy farm machinery to get to some of the animals. They examined any pig that would allow them to get close. But most ran in the opposite direction.

Lennon began shouting from the truck. "Sarah. Mom. That one. That one over there! I can see the pig limping behind the knocked-down feed shed."

The team turned to look at Lennon and saw her pointing to a far corner of the farm. They each saw the pig and began approaching her slowly from different directions. The closer they got, the more injuries they noticed. This pig had a cyst on her back hip the size of a softball, the cut on her ear was bleeding, and a puncture wound on the bottom of her hoof caused the limp.

Mel was the first to get to her and got on one knee. "We are here to help you."

The pig was too nervous and exhausted to run. She could barely walk. There was nothing she could do except let them help her.

Mel repeated, "We're here to help you and drive you to a beautiful home where you will live happily forever. You may not know what the word help means, but I promise you will because we will show you. But first, we must put this lead rope around your neck and get you to our van. Although it's a long walk, I believe you can do it. Our team will be right beside you the entire way. Once we are there, you can rest for hours with clean water and some food." The pig looked up with sad eyes. Then, they surrounded her with panels and guided her out of the yard. The panels helped her walk a straight line as the shortest distance was all she could walk in her condition.

The team was almost at the van when the farmer returned with a friend. "Not her. You're not taking her. That pig is my property. If you take her, you're stealing from me. Take that rope off her, or I will."

It was difficult, but Mel took some deep breaths, remained calm, and said to both men, "We agreed to take the most injured pig we could find. That is exactly what we are doing. She is practically unable to walk, and her hoof is terribly infected. Untreated, she could lose her ability to walk or even die."

The farmer didn't believe anything Mel was saying and kicked the panels out of her hands. The pig stood still, which was uncharacteristic. Usually, pigs run away fast any chance they get. But pigs are cognitively brilliant animals. She knew she was safe with them. The policeman saw the commotion and reminded the farmer of their agreement. Mel picked up her panel, and they all walked on.

"I swear, Mel, I almost yelled at them, and I'm pretty good, well, decent, at keeping my cool. It's amazing how people can see the same situation so differently. Humph, not even injured! What's that guy talking about?" Sarah vented.

"It is always best to remain calm. It is not about us and our egos. Our rescues are about animals. We get nowhere when we yell," Walker replied.

It took five of them to lift the pig up and put her comfortably into the van. Sarah jumped in, gave her pig food and water, and kissed her goodbye.

"It's time to roll out. Thank you for being here with us. I'll be in touch," Mel said.

Lennon hugged Sarah. "Bye, Sarah. Next time, I will drive your truck." Lennon then turned around to the backseat. "I love you, piggy. You are on your rescue ride." Mojo barked. They all watched the pig put her head down to rest.

Before they began their eight-hour drive to Colorado, Mel decided to start a fundraiser to help cover the pig's medical bills. She shared it on Instagram and Facebook and then drove off.

They drove into the sunset under a dark sky illuminated by millions of shimmering stars and finally made it to their destination as the sun began to reappear. Abigail arranged for a stall to be set up at Rocky Mountain Animal Hospital with doctors ready. When the van pulled in, Dr. Easton came out to greet them.

"Welcome. We've been waiting for you. I'm the pig's doctor. Let's see her." Dr. Easton opened the van doors, and the pig was in the corner. The pig didn't look well. She was very lethargic. Dr. Easton began nudging her body. The pig released several loud grunts. Getting her out of the van would be challenging, so Dr. Easton made a ramp out of two large animal stretchers and lined it with strawberries and Cheerios. About 15 minutes later, they all saw the pig limp down the ramp, eating treats along the way. Finally, in her stall, she found a comfortable spot in a bed of hay and began to rest.

"Cheerios work every time," Dr. Easton said to Lennon.

"For me too," Lennon responded while taking a handful out of the box for herself and Mojo to share. Then, Lennon walked over, pet the top of the pig's snout and threw some hay on her back. "Look, a hay blanket. I'm tired too," Lennon said.

"Yeah, it's been a long 24 hours for all. We will check into a nearby hotel to get some rest and come back to check in on her," Mel said.

Mel, Lennon, and Mojo woke up from their slumber, showered, and went to grab a bite. After they ordered, Mel checked the fundraiser. She couldn't believe her eyes. Thousands of dollars were donated. The story of the pig's rescue made it around the world as donations came from people living in Europe and Asia.

"Lennon, this is tremendous. I had no idea we could raise this much money in such a short period. Or that anyone would care enough about one pig to donate. With this money, we'll be able to cover all the medical bills and perform any surgery necessary to give her a second chance at living a wonderful life." Mel said.

"I'm done eating. Can we go see the pig now?" Lennon asked.

When they returned to the animal hospital, Dr. Easton was in her stall. "So, everyone wants to know. What are you going to name her?"

Lennon responded, "A Pig Named Love!"

Mel laughed and said, "Lennon, wow! That came really fast. How so?"

"Because everyone showed how much they loved her when they gave us money," Lennon answered.

"That is an interesting way to look at it. I think that name suits her. People we don't even know have shown her compassion, selflessness, and love. Such beautiful things can happen when we come together and act out of the kindness of our hearts. A Pig Named Love is her full name, Dr. Easton. Love surrounds her."

Dr. Easton replied, "That is the most beautiful name. She is very lucky. Today, we will remove the cyst on her back, treat the infected hoof and disinfect all her cuts. We have already run blood work and are waiting for the results. She was quite dehydrated, so we put an IV drip to replenish the electrolytes; that's the needle in her back. She has a long recovery, but we will do everything we can to ensure she gets a well-deserved second chance at life. I will coordinate with Abigail when she can pick her up and bring her to Country Roads Rescue. You guys did great work."

"Dr. Easton, she is a fighter. She will get through this. We are all so grateful to you and your team," Mel responded.

"Oh, before I forget, a local news network reached out to us after hearing her story on social media. Would you mind if their team comes in to do a feature on A Pig Named Love?" Dr. Easton asked.

"A Pig Named Love is going to be famous. That is so cool," Lennon shouted and danced.

"We would be honored to have her story aired on TV. And while we won't be in town to film it, I trust your team will tell the story right. Send me the clip so we can watch it too," Mel said.

Mojo walked up to A Pig Named Love and began licking and cleaning her. Even though she was exhausted and dirty from the farm, she was responsive to their visit by letting them pet and sit with her before they said their goodbyes.

On the way to the airport, Sarah called. "Checking in, got any good news on our girl?"

"She is doing great. Lennon named her A Pig Named Love. She has a long road ahead before feeling good, but the doctor seemed optimistic," Mel answered.

"Of course she did. It's a perfect name," Sarah said.

A year later, Mel, Lennon, and Mojo received a wedding invitation in the mail from Country Roads Animal Rescue, asking if they wanted to attend the marriage ceremony between A Pig Named Love and Buddy Hoggy. Delighted, they called Abigail for more details. Abigail told them the story.

"When A Pig Named Love arrived, our team tried assimilating her into the big herd of pigs. Despite her size, she kept getting bullied. Buddy Hoggy, also part of the big herd, saw what was happening to Love. He began to protect her. The two of them spent all their time together. Love at first sight. Then we had this idea that they should get married and live together in their own pen. So that is what we are doing. She deserves to be celebrated. Love deserves to be celebrated."

"That is incredible. We won't be able to attend, but we will place an order of fruit to be delivered from a local market for all to enjoy," she said.

Lennon took the phone out of Mel's hand. "And Cheerios! And Cheerios! She loves Cheerios."

Mel looked at Lennon and Mojo, "You know, we could only save one pig out of the millions left behind. But A Pig Named Love's story will inspire many to live with love and compassion. You guys did great work. That was a long and hard rescue. Emotionally and physically very challenging. Get your bathing suit on, and let's hit the beach. The sun sets soon. We have time for a swim in the ocean."

CHAPTER ~3~

Ollie

It was fall, and Moonlight Mile Ranch was in full bloom. The summer heat finally blew through, and the air was clean. June was in the field working. She had been taking courses in regenerative farming that is a farming method that uses nature's power to help achieve results. June dedicated a section of the ranch to harvesting tomatoes, squash, peppers, and more. Mel, Lennon, and Mojo were on a walk with Hickory. Lennon was now leading Hickory on her own while Mel and Mojo walked alongside them. When they made it to the end of the trail, Lennon noticed a donkey in the pasture.

"Who is that donkey?" asked Lennon.

"I believe that donkey belongs to Sherman, one of Slick's friends. She asked if we could keep him here for a few weeks, and I said yes. We have the space as Slick completed fencing for the small pasture that will eventually lead to the barn. Let's go introduce ourselves," Mel responded.

When they arrived, the donkey let out a very loud hee-haw, a sound known as a bray. Hickory nickered back.

Just then, a woman came out of the trailer, dusting herself off, and said, "I'm Sherman, Slick's friend. This is my guy. His name is Ollie. He's a two-year-old donkey."

Mel smiled. "I'm Mel. This is Lennon, Mojo, and Hickory. Moonlight Mile is our ranch. We are so happy that Ollie is here."

"Thank you for letting Ollie crash here. Slick and I go way back. I used to keep a rescue horse at Sagebrush until she passed away," Sherman said.

"Slick has told me so many wonderful things about you. It's our pleasure," Mel said.

"It feels good to be standing and moving around. I made my partner drive me to Texas, where I got Ollie. I picked him up at a livestock auction and paid seventy-five dollars for the little guy. Can you believe that! Seventy-five dollars." Sherman shook her head.

"I mean yes and no. That is not much money. I've heard of rescues purchasing donkeys for $250 or more. I guess many factors go into the price, including the condition and weight of the animal and how many meat buyers are in attendance. I've never been to a livestock auction. But if I were to go, I'm confident we'd return with a trailer full of equines and other farm animals. Grateful to you, Sherman. Ollie, like all horses and donkeys, deserves dignity and respect. You just gave him that," Mel commented.

"That's very kind of you. Yeah, it was my first auction. I won't ever do it again; it's gut-wrenching. But the good news is, I get to make sure Ollie thrives in his new life." Sherman sighed.

Lennon looked up and asked, "Sherman, what's a livestock auction?"

Sherman looked at Mel. "Listen, I say it like it is."

Mel responded, "Please, be honest."

Sherman bent down to Lennon's height. "I don't know how else to put this, except with the truth, which I believe you can handle at your age. At my age, we have a hard time with the truth. I am much older than you. A livestock auction is where people take their animals that are of no use to them. In some cases, that means show or competition horses that can't perform anymore, unwanted pets, sick animals, senior animals, or animals specifically bred for human consumption. Most animals at these auctions are horses, donkeys, pigs, cows, goats etc. No dogs. No cats. Humans tend to treat them with dignity. Now once the animals and the buyers are there, an auction begins. The highest bidder, the person willing to pay the most money, keeps the animal. The rules are simple. The attendees are mostly meat buyers and maybe some animal rescue organizations, like our team when we purchased Ollie. The meat buyers that win will then sell the equines to other parts of the world for food. Ollie was an unwanted pet. His owner surrendered him to a livestock dealer, and that dealer brought Ollie to market on the day our team showed up. And that is how it works. Some animals get lucky. Most don't. Any questions?"

"Umm, I don't have any questions. I feel angry." Lennon replied.

"Yeah, I get angry too. But I take that anger and transform it into something positive, like continuing to rescue animals. Lennon, you have to keep on keepin' on. That's what they say, and that is what I do. In the end, we'll have saved a lot of lives," Sherman said.

"Mom, let's rescue a horse or animal from one of those auctions. I think that would be a good idea," Lennon stated.

"Take my trailer. Get as many animals out as you can," Sherman chimed in.

"I promise to do that with you one day," Mel replied to Lennon.

"It's gross that people eat donkeys and horses," Lennon responded.

"To you, yes, but to others, it's food. Other cultures can judge the American diet, so it's best not to criticize anyone," Mel said.

"Ollie is cute," Lennon giggled.

"A total charmer. Look at his grey and white curly short hair, long fluffy ears, soft snout, and short tail. He's adorable." Mel smiled.

"He's thin and will need to put on weight. But he will always be a small donkey. Some donkeys can grow to be the size of a horse. Ollie will be the size of a miniature pony. My next step is to make sure I can place him in an incredible home. I was his ticket out. I'll keep him under my care until the right home comes along. I can't keep him forever, though, as I have too many of my own animals. Rescue is about being responsible. The animals that stay with me are the ones that are impossible to place as they come with too many health issues. I built out small spaces for each animal in my backyard. Henry, my goat. I drain his abscesses with my hands. It is like popping a massive cyst. Totally gross. Gilbert, the pig is horrendously overweight. His previous owners fed him beer and cereal. He can only walk a few steps at a time before toppling over. He is addicted to beer, so we are working on breaking that addiction. But this guy, Ollie, with a few more pounds and some love, he has a bright future," Sherman said.

"Sherman, do donkeys like dogs? Because Mojo just found a way into the pasture. Big Brother Mojo, what are you doing?" Lennon laughed.

"Oy. Donkeys don't usually like dogs. They remind them of coyotes. Mojo has really intense coyote energy and Mojo is running. Ollie is chasing him. I can't look," Sherman exclaimed.

Ollie continued to chase Mojo around the pasture. The two played with each other. Often, Mojo would look back to see where Ollie was, and most of the time he was right behind him, which sent Mojo running again. The two drank side by side at the water tank when they exhausted themselves. Finally, Mojo lay down to rest in the shady part of Ollie's pasture. Ollie curiously smelled Mojo, and often Mojo set a boundary by letting out a bark.

"What a remarkable connection! I didn't see that coming. I don't believe Ollie has ever seen a dog, let alone played with one. I love animal rescue. The work is hard, but the rewards are tremendous!" Sherman cheered.

"This is Mojo's first time playing with a donkey. He knows Hickory, but the two don't play. So Ollie has a new friend." Mel smiled.

"If Mojo is playing with Ollie, can I play with him too?" Lennon asked.

"Ollie and I would be grateful to your family if you did. He needs as much positive reinforcement and attention as possible. My donkey is your donkey. I mean, listen, he needs to decompress from his time at that feedlot. I know he carries trauma from living through that experience. So, be patient with him," Sherman responded.

"Will he be okay?" Lennon asked.

Sherman looked at Lennon. "Yes, Ollie will be okay. I know he'll live a wonderful life with his four new amazing friends. That's you guys. But before Ollie came to Moonlight Mile Ranch, his life was hard. He had little room to move, and he had to fight for morsels of food. He was never able to be happy and free."

"Sherman, are you a full-time animal rescue worker?" Mel asked.

"No, I run a dog grooming business. I do what I can," Sherman said.

Lennon interrupted the conversation, tugging at Sherman's shirt, and asked, "I need to know, what does Ollie eat?"

"He likes carrots. But cut them up into small pieces. He has a hard time chewing. He has a little mouth. He loves peppermint candies. Remember, don't put your hands in his mouth when you're with him. He'll think your fingers are carrots. And never get behind him. Donkeys can kick," Sherman said.

Mel chimed in, "We'll take great care of him. I rescue animals, too. We should talk about doing a rescue together in the future. Get home safely, and don't worry about him,"

Mel tied Hickory's lead rope to the fence outside Ollie's pasture and dropped some hay from Ollie's feeder on the ground for him to graze on. Mel and Lennon entered the pasture. Mojo came running over. Ollie didn't greet them the same way Mojo did. In fact, Ollie didn't greet them at all. He took a few steps in the opposite direction. His energy shifted, and he became reserved. Ollie didn't trust Mel or Lennon the same way he trusted Mojo and Sherman.

"Lennon, we can try sitting in his pasture to see if he'll approach us. If he doesn't, that's okay. He'll come to us when and if he is comfortable. Here, come sit next to me. Sitting and looking away from him shows the animals that we are not threatening," Mel said.

"Sherman gave me some carrots. I can see if he wants one," Lennon said.

"Sure. Remember, though, that this is a process. If we're patient, then one day, we'll be able to show him all the affection in the world. But, for now, we must respect his comfort levels," Mel said.

Mel, Lennon, and Mojo sat in the pasture with carrots on the ground, waiting for Ollie. They waited and waited. Ollie turned and walked to the far end of the pasture. He never ate the carrots.

"Listen, let's get out of his pasture. Ollie is here with us for a few weeks. So we have plenty of time to spend together. Tomorrow, we can pick up some peppermint candies. Maybe a sweet will help make him more trusting of us," Mel suggested.

"Only if I can eat them too," Lennon said.

"Sugar rush for all," Mel laughed.

The three left Ollie's pasture and walked Hickory back to his pasture. On the way, Lennon stopped to admire June's garden and noticed her tomatoes. "The tomatoes are beautiful. They are one of my favorite fruits," Lennon said. June and Lennon had become friends. June was inspiring Lennon to start a garden of her own. When they arrived, Lennon handed flakes of hay to Mel so she could throw them into the feeder for Hickory and his friend, Peanut.

Peanut was also a rescue horse. His mother, one of Mel's close friends, adopted him after being used as evidence in an animal cruelty case. He needed several surgeries. After his stay in the hospital, he came to Moonlight Mile to heal. His mother visited him daily; she absolutely adores him.

Mel woke Lennon and Mojo up the next morning and cooked them breakfast. As they ate, they heard a very, very loud hee-haw.

"That must be Ollie, letting us know he is hungry too," Mel laughed.

Mel and Lennon walked to the window to see the commotion. They saw Ollie talking to Hickory and Peanut. Hickory paid no attention. Peanut was curious and kept looking at Ollie from a distance and nickering back.

"I guess this is what it would be like if we rescued a rooster. They make a lot of morning noise, too," Lennon said while eating her toast.

"Funny. Let's hope he doesn't wake up at 6 am all the time," Mel responded. "Len, when you're done, get dressed, we'll drop some hay in the feeders for the boys, then go pick up some peppermint candy."

When they returned to the ranch, they walked into Ollie's pasture with peppermints and carrots and sat again in the middle of the field. They kept their distance like the day before.

"Hey Lennon, check it out. The carrots from yesterday are gone. Ollie ate them when we left his pasture. So today, let's try to get him to eat a treat when we are near him. We can't force a connection. We can't force anything, for that matter," Mel said as she gently tossed a carrot in Ollie's direction.

"Ollie ate the carrot. Throw another one," Lennon shouted.

Mel threw another carrot. Ollie took another step towards them to eat it.

"My turn to throw a carrot," Lennon said.

"Ollie is pretty close to us now. Try hand-feeding him one of the peppermint candies. Let's see if he takes it from you," Mel said.

Lennon reached into the bag, unwrapped two peppermint candies, and extended her arm towards Ollie. Ollie took a step, stretched his neck, and took the peppermint candies out of Lennon's hand.

"His lips are so soft. They tickled me." Lennon laughed.

"Great work, Lennon," Mel said.

Mel and Lennon fed Ollie for a bit longer.

"Today was awesome. We made progress. Let's end this session on a high and come back again. Where is Mojo?" Mel said.

As they walked out of Ollie's pasture, they saw Mojo snoozing near June's compost pile. "Mojo really loves poop. It's gross," Lennon said.

"I know. He smells so bad at the end of the day. I think he likes the way it tastes. I mean, he eats it all the time." Mel laughed.

"Mojo, come! No more poop for you today," Lennon shouted, who came running over. Mojo adored Lennon and listened to her more than he listened to Mel.

A few weeks later, Mel, Lennon, and Mojo decided to take Ollie on a walk as they noticed significant progress. Now, Ollie would run over to greet them. When they got down on their knees, Ollie would rest his big heavy head on their shoulders to give them hugs. He trusted Lennon when she patted his withers and scratched his chest. And he always let Mel kiss his lips. Then, it was time for the next step. Mel took a halter and lead rope out of the shed and walked to Ollie's pasture.

"Lennon and Mojo, you guys wait outside. I don't know how he will react to a halter around his head. This is new," Mel explained.

Mel went into the pasture with a few peppermints in her hand. Ollie came over to Mel and treated him to one candy as she tried to put the halter around his head. Ollie pulled away. The halter was new and scary, but the peppermints were delicious. He fought the halter momentarily, but Ollie wanted more treats in the end. So, he let Mel tie the halter and lead him out of the pasture.

"Len, I am going to hold the lead rope. He is so strong. I don't want him to pull you around," Mel said.

"Okay, but I am going to walk right here, next to you, to be safe and close to Ollie." Lennon pointed to the right side of Ollie.

Ollie began pulling Mel in all directions. First, he dragged her up the hill to eat the leaves on the trees. Then down the hill to munch on some long grass. And then along the trail to taste the fresh flowers. Thank goodness he didn't find June's garden. Otherwise, he would've eaten her entire harvest. Mojo thought this was awesome and began running with Ollie. Lennon laughed every time Mel was pulled in a new direction, quite frequently. Mel tried really hard but could not get Ollie to follow any direction. And while the four of them were out of the pasture for almost an hour, they never got far.

Mel, Lennon, and Mojo dedicated more time teaching Ollie how to walk on a lead rope. Ollie enjoyed his time out of the pasture and got better at taking directions. His favorite route was visiting Hickory and Peanut. Mel began introducing them by putting down some hay between the fence for all the boys to share. Their long noses touched, and often, Peanut would stretch his long neck over the fence and nip Ollie on the rear. Which would set Ollie off, and he would hee-haw back at him. Lennon found this most amusing. "Ollie makes the loudest sounds," she would say each time.

Soon enough, Hickory, Ollie, and Peanut were being turned out in an open pasture together. Hickory and Ollie would run alongside each other. Hickory taught Ollie attention, confidence, rhythm, and balance. Peanut, the same age as Ollie, taught him the importance of play, misbehaving, and rolling. Peanut's favorite game was biting the head of the hose every time Mel tried to clean their water tank. Ollie took to this quite quickly. The three were becoming a close herd.

The most rewarding moment for Mel and Lennon was when they took Hickory and Ollie on a hike up the steepest mountain on the ranch. This was a challenging climb, and the fact that they could do it together showed how far Ollie had come on his journey. Lennon led Hickory and set the pace. Mel led Ollie and followed behind. Mojo ran ahead of all. Hickory and Ollie were excellent at listening to directions on when to stop and graze.

When they reached the top of the mountain, they saw the rolling green hills. Hickory and Ollie let out a nicker. Mel, Lennon, and Mojo caught their breath and then sat down to rest. Hickory and Ollie stood close to them. Everyone had a snack and some water.

"Hickory and Ollie really love each other," Lennon said.

"Ollie really loves Peanut, too," Mel responded.

"Can Ollie live here? This way, he can play with Hickory and Peanut all the time," asked Lennon.

"I need to talk to Sherman and he's still her donkey, but I was thinking the same thing. They get along so well. I don't think I would even feel comfortable breaking up the herd at this point. In fact, I think Ollie should move into their pasture. Sherman is coming to the ranch tomorrow so that we can discuss then," Mel said.

The next day, Sherman stopped by the ranch.

"Sherman, we wanted to talk about Ollie. He has made such incredible progress. He fits in exceptionally well with the other horses, and we just adore him. If you haven't found him a home, would you consider letting us adopt him?" Mel asked.

"You know, great minds think alike. I've been here to check in on him a few times, and he has made incredible progress. But most of all, he's found joy and love. In Texas, I promised him a happier life. Moonlight Mile is where he'll have that security and love. I would be honored to have your family adopt him. Ollie, welcome home! I'm so glad I thought of this idea," Sherman said.

"Fantastic! Want to walk him to the big pasture so he can live with Hickory and Peanut," Mel said.

"Are you kidding me! Yes," Sherman said.

"Wanna hold the lead rope?" Lennon asked Sherman.

"Absolutely." Sherman took the lead rope, and they all walked to the horses.

"Ollie, you're going to be living with Peanut and Hickory. Peanut may bite you on the tush, but just nip him back if you have to," Lennon said to Ollie as they walked.

"That is wonderful advice. Guys, I can't believe how well Ollie is walking on a lead rope. At the auction, we had to push him into the trailer. I mean really exceptional work," Sherman laughed.

Mel opened the gate so Sherman could lead Ollie in. As Mel took off his halter, she bent down to kiss his nose. Ollie did what he always did and gave Mel a big, long donkey hug. Hickory and Peanut came storming down the mountain to greet him. They all started to play. Ollie kicked a few times at both horses. Peanut did try to bite his rear. Hickory chased them both off. Mel laughed and said to Lennon, "Ollie will be the leader of the herd. A donkey in charge of the horses."

Mel and Lennon threw the hay over the fence and into their feeder. The boys gathered around to eat a snack.

"Lennon, thank you for having so much patience with Ollie. Did you learn anything?" Mel asked Lennon.

"Second chances are important, and every animal in this pasture has had one," Lennon said.

"It is amazing what love and gentleness can do. To love is so simple," Mel said.

"Okay. This is getting too sappy for me. I am going to head home," Sherman interrupted.

"Bye, Sherm," Lennon shouted.

"You know what, Lennon? I love you, Mojo, Hickory, Peanut, and Ollie," Mel said.

"I love everyone too. Let's have Slick and June over for dinner tonight," Lennon suggested.

"Sounds good," Mel said, and they all walked back to the house together as the sun was setting over Moonlight Mile Ranch.

CHAPTER ~4~

The Poets

Mel, Lennon, and Mojo were hanging out at the Malibu Pier, enjoying their breakfast of scones and coffee, looking out at the surfers catch the long smooth waves this cove was known for when Mel received a call from Sherman.

"Sherman, what's going on!" Mel said excitedly.

"No time for chit-chat. What are you doing?" Sherman quickly said with an unsettled tone. A tone very typical of Sherman as she always had something going on and, most of the time, it was urgent.

"Taking the morning off, relaxing," Mel replied.

"Sherman," Lennon shouted into the phone.

"I know I said no time for chit-chat, but what's that kid doing? Is she riding Hickory yet?" Sherman asked.

"We're taking our time getting there. I want her to be comfortable with him and vice-versa. She's taking her brother Hickory for long trail walks. Progress has been made, and all is good," Mel said.

"Now down to business. I need you to check out a private residence in Malibu. Some family with a ton of land has neglected their animals. I'm not sure of the conditions or the actual story. I'm sending you a woman's phone number who can get you on the site. Her name is Anna. She works with the family that owns the property," Sherman said.

"Interesting. Are you going to meet me there? What kind of animals should I expect?" Mel asked.

"Nah, I can't get out of the shop. I'm swamped with grooming appointments. And I may have to save twelve pheasants this afternoon. Don't ask. People! You are on your own for this one. Let me know how it goes." Sherman hung up.

Mel took her last sip of coffee and called Anna. They spoke for several minutes and planned on a visit that afternoon. The ranch wasn't too far from where they were. The drive through the mountains was lovely. When they arrived at the gate, Anna buzzed them in and told them to follow the road all the way. She'd be waiting. The road to the top was narrow and steep. On every sharp turn, Lennon would say, "Whoaaa," from the back seat. It was unclear to Mel how any trailer made it up there in the first place. When the mountain finally plateaued, Mel parked the truck, and they all got out.

"Anna. This is Lennon and Mojo. This property is massive. Tell us what is going on," Mel said.

"Nice to meet you guys. My mom and I have been working on this property for years. The owner is our boss. He lives here half the year, maybe less. I oversee the property to make sure nothing bad happens while he's away. The family has allowed my mom and me to acquire animals over the years and keep them on site as long as we oversee their care. The issue now, we are moving out of state. I can't leave our animals here. I need to re-home them before leaving this job. The only animals that will stay on the property are the goats that belong to the owner. And a Texas Longhorn bull that roams the mountains. You may see him, but mostly, he keeps to himself. As you can see, the property is huge, but it is all fenced in, so he is free to roam," Anna responded.

"A Texas Longhorn in California? That's silly. Why do you have so many goats?" Lennon asked.

"The workers have a spot where they drop hay and fill up a water bin at the mountain's base, so the Longhorn is never hungry or dehydrated. The goats help with brush clearance. They eat the mustard plants that grow rampant on the hillside. These highly combustible plants flourish in Malibu, putting the property at high risk during fire season. It's wild how the goats love to eat the plants and seeds. They are so effective as they eat the entire plant. Lawnmowers don't compare as they leave the roots and seeds behind, only to grow again. They are not used for agriculture of any kind," Anna commented.

"All over California, people are using goats for fire abatement. The wildfires have been out of control these past few years. It makes sense. So, the goats and the longhorn are staying here. Then what animals on-site need to be re-homed?" Mel asked.

"Two alpacas and two dogs. Those are our pets," Anna answered.

"Before I set eyes on the animals, are you comfortable transferring ownership to me?" Mel said.

"Happy to sign any documents. Whatever you need to keep this clean," Anna replied.

"Then let's all take a walk around," Mel said.

Mel, Lennon, Mojo, and Anna began to walk to the first pasture.

"Mom, I don't know what it is, but something here feels eerie," Lennon whispered.

"I agree, Lennon. Something isn't right. It's essential to trust that intuition while on a rescue. Stay close to me. I'll protect you and brother Mojo," Mel responded.

When they arrived, Anna began to open the gate. It made a screeching noise. Just then, a large Anatolian Shepard came sprinting over from the far end of the pasture. This breed is commonly used on farms as they are meant to protect herds of goats, sheep, and pigs from larger predators such as mountain lions and coyotes. But this guy was different. He wasn't intimidating, even though he was easily over 120 pounds with a loud bark and sharp teeth. His run was goofy, more like a skip hop. His fur was dirty and in need of a wash. His face had cuts on his nose from the wire fencing. He looked beaten up. Mojo's natural response was to begin to bark back. And soon, two dogs were barking loudly while wagging their tails and sniffing each other.

"Lennon, Mojo, even though this dog appears friendly, I'll have you two wait outside the pasture. Remember, we are entering into his space as strangers. He may be very protective, and any miscommunication may lead to an injury we would all rather avoid," Mel suggested.

"Okay, Mom. I'll keep an eye on big brother Mojo. He always misbehaves." Lennon took hold of Mojo's leash and began petting his head.

"This is Hank. He is super friendly. Hank is one of the dogs that needs to be re-homed. He is maybe five years old and would need an outdoor space as he has lived on a farm his entire life," Anna said.

"Noted," Mel said as she bent over to pet him.

Anna led Mel to a makeshift shelter. Wooden beams held the structure together, while grey and blue tarp and duck tape created walls and a roof. When Mel entered, the smell was so potent that her eyes began to burn, blinding her for a moment. The scent was an accumulation of animal urine. It was strong like ammonia and sat thick in the air as the shelter lacked ventilation. Once Mel acclimated to the smell, she was able to look around. The water tanks were empty, cobwebs hung from the ceiling, and flies were everywhere as they were attracted to urine, and damp hay lay on the ground. In a corner, she spotted another dog, also an Anatolian Shepard, who looked exactly like Hank.

"That is Seymour, Hank's sister. She isn't nice. Seymour is the second dog that needs to be re-homed. They should be placed together as they are bonded," Anna said.

Mel observed Seymour as she sat still in a dark, hot corner, letting flies bite her skin. She was defeated.

"Seymour. I'm here to find you a new home. Living inside this shelter isn't the life you were meant to live. I can see how badly you need a bath and proper food. Those knots must be pulling at your skin. I know your brother has adapted to his surroundings differently than you. And that is okay as we each experience events differently. I'll be back to get you out of here. I promise," Mel whispered to her.

No other animals were in the shelter, so Mel and Anna decided to move on. On the way out, Mel was met by a large white furry alpaca staring at her.

"We were just looking for you, mister. I know he looks cute, but he has been hostile since we separated him from his friend. This is one of the alpacas that needs a home," Anna said.

The alpaca stared at Mel. When she took a step to the right, the alpaca followed her with his eyes. Then, all of a sudden, the alpaca showed his teeth and spit. The spit landed right on Mel's chest.

"Are you okay?" Anna asked.

"Yes, I'm fine. It's not the first time, and it won't be the last that an alpaca spits on me. It's just gross every time. I know they spit to protect themselves. He doesn't want us in his space. That was his warning," Mel said, trying to wipe alpaca saliva off her shirt.

The alpaca took off and ran over to the fence. Then, he started to pace back and forth, screeching and jumping up on his hind legs.

"Okay, so more details on the alpacas. Why did you separate them?" Mel asked.

"I didn't. The workers did. Not sure why we never brought them back together," Anna replied.

"What are the alpacas' names?" Mel asked

"We never named them. They are both 15 years old. We got the boys when they were six years old," Anna said.

"You never named them? Where is the second alpaca?" Mel asked.

"He is in the next pasture. Most likely behind that wooden shed. Where he always is." Anna pointed.

Hank followed Mel to the gate as she left the pasture. Mel then checked in on Lennon and Mojo.

"Mom, don't come over to me. You smell. I saw him spit on you. It is all over you. That was gross. He's still trying to jump over the fence," Lennon replied.

Mojo liked the smell and jumped up on Mel to lick it off her.

"No licking, Mojo. The alpaca was separated from his friend for who knows how long. I would be upset too. I'm going to check on the second alpaca. I still think it's too dangerous to have you in the pasture, so I want you here in a safe space," Mel said.

"Mojo and I are hanging out under the orange tree and watching the goats," Lennon commented.

"Lennon, do you want me to grab a ladder, and we can pick some fruit off the top of the tree?" Anna chimed in.

"Yes," Lennon answered.

"Awesome. Shout for me if you need anything," Mel said.

Knowing how angry the first alpaca was, Mel didn't know what to expect meeting the second alpaca. She walked around to the back of the wooden shed, and there he was, lying on the ground. Mel dropped to her knees at the sight of him. He was very skinny.

His white fleece was black from all the dust and lack of shearing. When he turned his head to see who was there, Mel saw hundreds of flies in his eyes and swarming around his head. While on the ground, Mel tried to inspect his body, but it was no use. His fleece was too thick. Mel began talking to him in a soft, calming voice. "We are going to get you out of here. I promise to find a vet that will help heal your eyes. You must be in so much pain. I promise you a wonderful life. This treatment or lack of tending to your needs will never happen to you again." Mel got up, dusted her jeans, and walked over to the orange tree.

"So, how is the orange-picking going?" Mel questioned when she arrived back at the group.

"Look how many we have," Lennon said as she showed Mel half a bucket full of oranges.

"Your face looks sticky. Have you been eating them too?" Mel laughed.

"Yup," Lennon said as she peeled another one.

"California grown. Like you." Mel smiled and then turned to Anna. "Anna, it is critical that I immediately take the alpacas off the property. I will need the night to make arrangements. I need you to be here tomorrow as this can't wait another day. Have you seen the flies in the second alpaca's eyes?" Mel questioned.

"I was aware of the problem. We tried to put a fly mask on him months ago, but he wouldn't let us. So my mom and I just left it as is. Tomorrow works," Anna replied.

"Anna, rescuing an animal is a selfless act of honor and courage. But when you rescue an animal, you need to be able to take care of them for the duration of their life. You commit to that animal. That commitment means providing food, proper shelter, medical care and love. The second alpaca has flies burrowing in his eyes. You have known about this for months. He could lose his vision because of your inability to act. If a fly mask doesn't work, there is fly spray, or you could hang fly traps around the wooden shed to deter insects. A vet should have been brought in months ago to see what was happening. If these animals are your pets, then you must be tuned into their needs. And if you are unable to provide those basic needs, you need to call for help. Sherman and I should have received this call a long time ago. When was the last time a vet came out?" Mel said sternly.

"We used to have a vet come out. We can't afford it anymore. It's been over two years since their last health check. I was too proud, and so was my mom, to admit we couldn't handle it. I'm trying to do the right thing now," Anna said.

"What you and your mother did was not right. These animals didn't ask you to rescue them, but when you did, they relied on you to care for their basic needs. This could have been prevented with basic vet care every few months at a minimal cost. Heck, I am not even sure we'll be able to save that one alpaca's vison," Mel said as she opened the truck doors so Lennon and Mojo could get in.

"Mom, is the second alpaca really bad?" Lennon asked.

"Yeah, he is. You will see them tomorrow when they are both in the trailer. We will find them a forever home and get them whatever medical treatment they need," Mel said as she drove down the mountain.

"That is what we do. We help the animals. We will help these guys too," Lennon said while taking off her dusty sneakers and socks in the backseat.

When they arrived home, Mel changed her shirt, poured two glasses of water, and sat on the couch. Mel called Sherman to let her know about the conditions on the property and the animals. Sherman was appalled but not shocked. Nothing ever shocked Sherman as she was in animal rescue for far too many years. She saw it all and agreed to go to the farm tomorrow to pick up Hank and Seymour. She was looking for rescued dogs to protect the small animal herd at home. Due to lack of space, Sherman couldn't home large animals such as horses or donkeys. Mel was relieved, knowing that Hank and Seymour would have a purpose and mostly be spoiled with love for the rest of their lives.

"Hey, Lennon, what rescues do we know that have or had alpacas? We need to find them a home that knows what they are doing. Moonlight Mile isn't equipped for these two. We need someone that knows alpacas. These guys are in bad shape," Mel said, sipping water.

"Olivia had alpacas at her school. They were cute. I took pictures on your phone," Lennon remarked.

"Lennon. That's right. Olivia. Let's call her. She'll be honest if they can't take on the alpacas." Mel called Olivia. "Olivia, how are you?" Mel said.

"Mel. We miss you guys. How are you?" Olivia said.

"Overall, great. Right now, we are in the middle of a rescue. We have two alpacas that need a forever home. We are picking them up from a property in Malibu tomorrow. Even though they lived in a nice neighborhood, they were not kept in good condition. Lennon remembered that you had alpacas. Is that still the case? Do you have room for two more?" Mel asked.

"Oh my gosh. What perfect timing! We just completed a new pasture. Our alpacas passed away, and we have wanted to rescue new ones. We would love to take them. We will begin setting up the space for their arrival. I'll call the vet and make sure she can be here when you arrive," Olivia said.

"I appreciate you taking them in on such short notice. This is an emergency. I'll fill you in tomorrow when we drop them off." Mel hung up the phone.

Tomorrow came quickly, and they knew they had a busy day ahead. After breakfast, Lennon loaded up the truck with water and snacks for themselves while Mel attached the trailer to the truck. Lennon threw hay into the trailer, filled the water jugs , and grabbed two alpaca halters with lead ropes. The three of them were set and on their way to the property. When they arrived, Anna buzzed them in. Mel drove the truck slowly as the turns seemed even more narrow and sharp with a trailer attached. When they made it to the top, Anna waited by the two alpaca pastures. Mel pulled right in front. She got out and opened the trailer doors. Mojo then jumped out of the truck, and Lennon climbed out too.

"Good morning, Anna. I think we should get the more aggressive alpaca into the trailer first," Mel said.

"Sounds good," Anna answered.

"We brought halters, lead ropes, and lassos to use," Mel commented.

Lennon ran into the trailer and grabbed a lasso. Mel thanked Lennon for being so helpful. Lennon and Mojo walked back to the orange trees and kept themselves busy. Mel and Anna went into the pasture. The alpaca was nowhere in sight. They began to walk to the shelter. When they arrived, Mel put a bandana over her face to avoid the smell and stuck her head inside.

"Found him," Mel exclaimed.

The two tried to move the alpaca into a dark corner, closing in on him. If they could get close enough, they could get a lasso around his neck. But he stomped his forelegs and turned his butt to them to keep them from getting close. Mel moved in quickly and tried to get as close as she could and attempted to put the lasso around his neck. But the alpaca was too fast, and he ran out of the shelter. Mel fell to the ground, missing him completely.

"It was a good first try." Anna laughed.

"I think so. Where did he go?" Mel said while dusting herself off.

"For a quick guy, he didn't go far. He's outside the shelter, waiting to see what we will do next," Anna said, facing him.

"I'll approach slower with patience this time. A method that usually works with the animals," Mel exclaimed.

"I'll hang back so he doesn't feel that we're bullying him. I would also like to avoid getting spit on. I'm wearing a new shirt today." Anna smiled.

"That's great, Anna," Mel said and took a knee to show the alpaca that she was not a threat.

Mel waited. So did the alpaca. Then she stood up and reached her arm out. He stood there, too. While they were standing, looking at each other, Mel tossed the lasso, and it went around his neck. He pulled back. Mel was able to hold onto the rope. She held the lasso tight until he settled down. Then she led him out of the pasture and to the trailer.

"Great catch, Mom. No spit this time," Lennon shouted.

As they neared the trailer ramp, the alpaca decided to sit down with all four legs tucked under his body, making it impossible to move him forward. Mel tried to push him from behind, pull him forward, and even got next to him to nudge the side of his body. Nothing. He was dead weight.

"A protest! Take some oranges, Mom. They are sweet. I think he will love them. Then, I'll make a trail into the trailer. Just like we did with A Pig Named Love," Lennon suggested.

"Great idea," Anna replied.

Lennon laid a trail of oranges going into the trailer and threw the alpaca one so he could taste it. The alpaca took a bite, and his mood changed quickly. First, he blissfully ate the entire orange and looked around for another one. Then, he got up and took a few steps toward the next orange. He ate that one with just as much joy as the first. And so on until he found himself in the trailer, swallowing an orange and then peacefully grazing on the hay. Mel tied his lead rope to a hook inside the trailer to secure him so he didn't get hurt in transit. As Mel was securing the rope, the alpaca looked at Mel, and even though he was comfortable in the trailer, spit on her anyway.

"Well, I think he just enjoys spitting on me. This could be his thing, you know. Lennon, keep an eye on him from the trailers escape door. If he wants more oranges, feed them to him. I need to keep him calm and busy for as long as possible while I get the second alpaca loaded. He's secure in the trailer, so you're safe. Just don't go inside," Mel said, wiping off her shirt.

Mel found the second alpaca in the same condition as when they first met. Mel kneeled to be at eye level with him. She put the lasso around his neck, peeled off a piece of orange, and gave it to him. They sat there while he ate it. She broke off another piece and gave it to him before asking him to get up. He ate the second piece. Mel stood up and gave a soft tug on the rope. He got up without a fight. She gave him another piece of orange, and the two walked together to the gate and into the trailer. In the trailer, he lay down on all four legs. The first alpaca began to cluck with joy that his friend was near him again. But the second alpaca just lay there. Lennon fed him oranges and moved the water bin closer to his mouth so he didn't need to work as hard to get it.

Mel closed the trailer doors, and Mojo and Lennon jumped into the truck. Before Mel pulled away, she let Anna know that Sherman was on her way to pick up the dogs and bring them to her home. Anna agreed to wait. When they reached the bottom of the mountain, Mel took a breath of relief and called Olivia to let her know they were on their way. Everyone was so excited that the alpacas were finally on their rescue ride to their new home.

"Hey, Lennon, what should we listen to? I was thinking Bob Dylan," Mel asked.

"Nah. We always listen to Bob. Put America on," Lennon replied.

"You want to listen to Allen Ginsberg again? This is the fourteenth time today we're listening to his poetry." Mel laughed.

"America, I've given you my all," Lennon shouted from the backseat.

"I think we may need to name one of the alpacas as Allen Ginsberg to celebrate this moment. And also that you know Beatnik poetry at such a young age." Mel shook her head.

"Yes. The little alpaca is going to be called Allen Ginsberg. I love it!" Lennon confirmed.

"So, what's the first alpaca going to be named?" Mel asked.

"Spithead," Lennon suggested.

"Very funny. Give me another suggestion. It has to go with Allen Ginsberg," Mel commented.

"Who writes all the books we have in the house? You are always reading them," Lennon asked.

"Charles Bukowski!" Mel shouted.

"Yes, that's it! Charles and Allen." Lennon giggled.

"Ladies and gentlemen, introducing Charles Bukowski and Allen Ginsberg. It is so good." Mel laughed. Mojo turned around to look at Lennon in the backseat and then at Mel driving and then decided to stick his head out the window for the remainder of the ride while Mel and Lennon recited Howl and America.

Olivia and her team were waiting outside when Mel pulled into the rescue. A quarantine unit was separated from the other animals for the two alpacas to decompress. Mel opened the trailer gate while Olivia opened the quarantine unit. Rick, one of the staff members, took the lead ropes and walked the alpacas out of the trailer and into the quarantine unit. The first alpaca ran around, taking in his new surroundings, while the other stood in the corner. Several goats came running over to see who the new animals were.

"Here they are! The big one is tough. Put up a real good fight getting into the trailer. He calmed down when he saw his friend. The weaker one loaded into the trailer easily and followed me without hesitation. We discovered they both love oranges, which explains why their mouths look discoloured. Is the vet here?" Mel asked.

"Oh boy. Look at them. They're in rough shape but beautiful. I'm so happy they're here. We have plenty of treats, and we can add oranges into the mix. The vet should be here any minute. Do they have names?" Olivia asked.

"Charles Bukowski is the bigger one. Allen Ginsberg is the smaller one. The names may seem peculiar, but they're not. Lennon and I have been reciting America by Ginsberg in the car. At home, I teach her about the Beat Generation of writers, which is easy to do when living in Los Angeles. We love books. The work of these two writers is present in our home. Maybe naming the alpacas after them will inspire a new Beat Generation of readers, maybe writers. Poetry isn't dead after all," Mel explained

"Brilliant. I absolutely love it. We haven't had any poets yet. Let alone any LA-based writer. Isn't that right, Charles. Oh, perfect timing. The vet just pulled up. Ruby, come over here. I want you to meet our new literary greats," Olivia shouted.

Ruby walked over and was introduced to Mel, Lennon, Mojo, Charles Bukowski, and Allen Ginsberg. Mel told Ruby their story and the conditions of the property. Ruby was saddened to hear the details but happy that the alpacas were rescued. She entered the quarantine unit and began her medical check on each alpaca. Allen let the vet inspect his eyes and body while Charles ran around in circles. Eventually, Mel had to go into the quarantine unit to hold Charles against the fence for the vet to examine him.

About an hour later, Ruby gave Mel and Olivia their diagnoses.

"Allen needs to have surgery for entropion in both eyes. We need to clean out the fly larva from his eyes and reposition his eyelids as they grew inward. Charles has an infected lump under his jaw that needs to be removed. Not sure what caused it, but most likely an infection that went untreated. They both need haircuts, vaccinations, toe trims, and teeth trims. I know this sounds like a lot, which it is, but both alpacas will go on to live healthy lives. Their physical wounds will recover quicker than their emotional ones. The trauma we don't see usually takes the longest to heal. So be patient," Ruby said.

"Wow. I have no words other than I am incredibly grateful to Olivia for taking in these two amazing boys and giving them a second chance. I'm also glad we got them off that property. I get frustrated when neglect such as this could have been avoided. But they're here now. Olivia, I will, of course, help pay for medical. But, I understand how expensive it is for a rescue to onboard one animal, let alone two," Mel said.

"Aww, I appreciate you, Mel. And Ruby, where would we be without you! Once Charles and Allen are healthy and strong, I'll put them into their pasture. These two will be great." Olivia smiled.

"I know. Now, if I can only find Lennon and Mojo." Mel laughed.

"I see them both in the pig pool. They look pretty dirty." Olivia smiled.

Mel walked over to the pig pool and laughed. "Come on, guys. I think a shower is in order when we get home."

"Mom, I love the piggies so much. Can we come back to see Charles and Allen?" Lennon asked.

"Sure can. Get your brother Mojo and let's go home. It's been a long and great day," Mel shouted.

The three of them walked to the truck, got in, and drove down the dirt road. The sun was setting over Olivia's property, and a new life officially began for Charles Bukowski and Allen Ginsberg.

Later, Mel saw she had missed a call from Sherman. She left a voice message. "So, I went to the property to pick up the dogs just after you left. They were a filthy mess. It's good that I'm a talented dog groomer, and my skillset came in handy for these two. Anyway, they're clean and about to be fed their dinner with me. The vet should be here tomorrow to ensure the dogs are in good health. Once cleared, I'll introduce them to the herd of animals. Oh, did you know there is a Texas Longhorn on that mountain! What is wrong with people. This is ridiculous. Okay, talk to you soon. Bye."

Weeks later, Mel, Lennon, and Mojo visited Charles and Allen. Charles had two surgeries to remove the lump in his throat and was doing well in a pasture with the goats and sheep. Allen had four eye surgeries. The vet saved his vision. He, too, was in the pasture with Charles. Both came to Olivia's, scared of humans, and were now eating grapes and apples out of volunteer hands. When

Mel walked over to say goodbye to Charles, he took one look at her and, without warning, spit in her face.

"Come on, Charles! This is ridiculous already. Every time," Mel said while wiping the spit off her glasses. Lennon laughed.

Olivia mentioned, "You know, you are the only person he does that to. He doesn't even do that to the vet or the person that shears his fleece. It's kinda amazing. Not sure what to make of it."

"Not that amazing for me. It is so wonderful to see them thriving. Thank you for your hard work. We'll be back to visit them soon," Mel said with a smile on her face.

"We can't wait to have you," Olivia said, giving them all a hug goodbye.

Lennon started to laugh again when they were all strapped in and ready to go. "It is so funny that he spits on you and that Mojo tries to lick it every time we see Charles. That's three spits already."

"It is disgusting. And just the beginning as Charles hasn't seen the end of me. At some point, we may lose track," Mel noted.

The truck pulled out of Olivia's driveway. The sun beamed down on the boulders that surrounded her home. Mel turned up the volume on the radio, and there he was again. Allen Ginsberg's voice, "The weight of the world is love …."

"You know what this poem is about, Lennon? It's about love and how love conquers all. In the end, it's all that matters. To love unconditionally." Mel smiled.

CHAPTER ~5~

Legends

It was a sunny spring afternoon at Moonlight Mile Ranch.
Lennon took June's advice and began gardening on her own. She
turned the soil to grow squash in anticipation of a beautiful fall
harvest. Mojo was sunbathing in the pasture next to his brother

Hickory. Occasionally, Lennon or Mel would check on them to ensure they weren't overheating in the sun. Either Hickory or Mojo would lift his head and then put it back down on the hot dirt to let them know they were happy.

Mel suggested to Lennon that they stop for a break. They grabbed their lunch bag from the cooler and settled under the giant oak tree. As they opened their bag, Ollie and Peanut came over to see what they were eating. Avocado sandwiches didn't appeal to them, so they continued grazing on grass. Lennon noticed a car driving down the dirt road. They weren't expecting any visitors. The car parked near their pasture, and a woman got out. It was Amy, a close friend. She was not in animal rescue but connected to the rescue community as she had her rescue dogs living in Malibu.

"Hey, guys," Amy shouted from the car.

"Hey, Amy. Come on up and sit with us," Mel shouted back.

Amy walked into the pasture with a bag of carrots for the horses and Mojo. Mojo believed he, too, was a horse and never missed an opportunity to share their treats.

"I had a feeling you guys would be here. Lennon, your garden looks lovely. But now is not the time for chit-chat. Six pigs will be euthanized tomorrow afternoon at a shelter in San Bernardino. Joan Didion wrote about San Bernardino in one of her books. She said it's a certain alien kind of place. I'm not sure what goes on there, but I don't like it. So, when the time comes, Lennon, I'll introduce you to Joan Didion. But not today. Today, we must talk about these pigs that were left behind after their owners were evicted. They were left without food and water for days before Animal Control showed up," Amy said as she hand-fed the carrots to Ollie, Hickory, Peanut, and Mojo.

"What does euthanize mean?" asked Lennon.

"It's a humane way of helping an animal pass away. Euthanizing animals that are not adopted is a way for shelters to regulate the surplus of unwanted pets. That includes dogs, cats, and even farm animals like these pigs. This is why we encourage people to adopt from shelters and not shop from breeders. So many amazing animals are waiting for a home," Mel answered.

"Well, we can't let this happen," Lennon exclaimed.

"This is why you are just so smart, Lennon. You see things the way I see things. I knew you would understand, which is why I came here first," Amy piped.

"I've been hearing so many stories of these pigs being surrendered or dumped at shelters. It has become a real problem for rescues in Southern California as they've run out of room. It's a complex issue. On the one hand, some people don't know what they're doing, pretending to be breeders. On the other hand, they overbreed, and their pigs develop a bad temperament or come with a ton of health issues. This makes them hard to adopt, and then they get dumped. And then there are social media influencers who post pictures of their pet pigs, and then everyone wants a piglet. The breeders will sell an animal to just about anyone that shows up with cash. People that buy these piglets think they're cute. But piglets become pigs. It's a real problem that only worsens," Mel vented.

"We can carry on. Or we can go get these pigs. Rescue is mostly cleaning up other people's messes," Amy said.

"That's the truth," Mel commented.

"Listen, if we can save A Pig Named Love, then we can save these guys too." Lennon put her hands on Mel's face to prevent more ranting.

"I'm just going to say it, rescuing these guys won't solve the bigger societal problem, but it will matter to this group of six. And I'm willing to do that. Amy, take it away and tell us everything you know," Mel said.

"Come gather around. I have a video of the property they were taken from. So, there are two boys and four girls. I believe one of them is pregnant, but who knows. They are adorable," Amy said as she played the video on her phone for Mel and Lennon.

The video showed broken-down structures, empty food, water bowls, and large metal scraps all over the ground. The scraps looked like parts that fell off a car or machine and were never put back on. It was clear that this home had transformed into a junk yard with pigs that happened to live there. The pigs squealed loudly and scurried from corner to corner to avoid anyone that took a step towards them. The video cut off when Animal Control entered the property.

"Ugh. The conditions look terrible, but the pigs look okay. Nothing noticeable stands out in that video that would alarm me. Such as a limp, external injuries, or terrible skin conditions," Mel said, relieved.

"I thought the same thing," Amy confirmed.

"Are there any other rescues involved in getting these pigs out of the shelter? I don't want to overlap efforts," Mel asked.

"No one else is involved in this rescue mission. Most rescues or sanctuaries in Southern California are at capacity. They had to say no. A mighty and important word, Lennon," Amy answered.

"I get it. What is their status at the shelter?" Mel asked

"The shelter pushed the animals to a red list. Which is why I'm here. Urging you to take them," Amy responded.

"Red is my favorite color. What does red-listed mean?" Lennon asked.

"The red-listed animals are in danger of being euthanized. Basically, they are next in line. This happens to the animals that were there for some time and were not claimed or adopted. It costs money to keep animals at shelters," Mel responded.

"What is the difference between A Pig Named Love and these pigs? These pigs do look smaller," Lennon questioned.

"There are many different kinds of pigs. A Pig Named Love is a farm hog. They can grow to be 700 pounds. They're bred specifically for human consumption. These pigs are sometimes called mini-pigs or micro mini pigs by breeders to sell the pigs. There is no such thing as a mini pig. These guys are pot-belly pigs. They are smaller but can still grow to be 150-200 pounds," Mel explained.

"That's not mini! We need to bring them to Moonlight Mile Ranch," Lennon exclaimed.

"If we brought them here, they could stay temporarily in the barn stalls that Slick finished. However, the barn needs work, and I definitely don't feel safe with piglets running around. We'll need to find them homes, but we can get them out of the shelter. Lennon, you and I will hit the feed store and pick up some hay bales and pig food. Amy, can you coordinate with the shelter, tell them we'll be there tomorrow while we set up the ranch, and get our truck ready for transport?" Mel said.

"I'll take care of all the logistics. Best news. I am so excited." Amy danced back to her car. The horses followed her to the pasture gate, looking for more treats. She gave them the rest of the bag.

Mel and Lennon finished their lunch and put away their gardening tools. They walked up to Slick's Airstream to inform him and June of the pigs coming to Moonlight Mile. They were overjoyed and loved the idea of more animals.

The following day, they loaded up the truck and trailer and began their two-hour drive to the shelter. When they arrived, they were escorted to the back where the farm animals were being held. Mel parked the trailer, and they all got out. The pigs' stall was clean. There was plenty of food, water, and shelter.

"I am here to pick up the pigs. Thank goodness, I see that males and females are separated to prevent more pregnancies. I heard at least one is pregnant," Mel said to one of the guards.

"Yeah, so um, these are them. I am not sure which one is pregnant, but I also heard that. Need help putting them into your trailer?" the guard asked.

"Nah, I got it. Not my first time rounding up pigs. Thank you, though." Mel laughed and showed the guard some scars on her arms. Mel entered the boys' stall. The two were very fast. They ran to all four corners of the stall to avoid being caught. Mel was exhausted but eventually managed to get a collar around the heavier pig. He was approximately 60 pounds with grey and white hair. He didn't squeal, but he moved his body around like crazy, making it difficult for Mel to carry him. Despite his efforts, she managed to get him into the trailer. The second pig knew it was his turn and hunkered down to the ground to make himself heavier and harder to lift. He was lighter, maybe 40 pounds, with grey and white hair. Mel picked him up without a problem. Once in Mel's arms, he relaxed as he just wanted to be with his best friend again.

Mel created a divide in the trailer to keep the boys separate from the girls. Then she entered the female stall. After watching what happened to the boys, all four began squealing and scurrying. A pig's squeal is one of the most upsetting sounds. It is high-pitched and deafening. It is meant to keep predators away. Unfortunately for these four, Mel was used to it, and the noise didn't distract her from getting them into the trailer. The girls weren't hard to catch, just very vocal. Once all the pigs were loaded, Mel, Lennon, and Mojo got into the truck and drove away. Mel was relieved that the pick-up was quick and successful.

"Mom, this is so fun. One of the girls was so small. The boys were big. I think I know which one is pregnant. Her belly looked huge. Like mine after ice cream," Lennon joyfully spoke while patting her belly with her hands.

"I noticed that too, Lennon. One was super small. I was careful, lifting all the female pigs if we had more than one pregnancy on our hands, which is likely. But, hey, there is something exceptional about this group. I liked their energy. I'm happy we rescued them," Mel said.

"Me too. The more snouts, the better. Hey, this is their rescue ride. We always play a song as we pull out of the shelters. What is their song going to be?" Lennon smiled.

Mel rolled down the windows for fresh air; *Shining Brightly* by Bob Seger was on their shuffle. "Here you go. This is a great lyric. *'The dark clouds are rollin' away, and oh, it's shining brightly, And I think it's all gonna be okay.* A fitting lyric for all the pigs in the back." Mel sang and wiped the sweat off her forehead.

"Mom, you look like John Denver. I love *Annie's Song*. Let's name one John Denver. Put that song on next," Lennon suggested.

"I'll take it as a compliment, I guess. John Denver, it is. How about John Denver and Jim Morrison for the boys?" Mel laughed.

"*L.A. Woman* is Mojo's song. Jim sings it. Put Mojo's song on next, Mojo, your song is coming on," Lennon shouted. The radio in the truck played a mix of John Denver, The Doors, and some other 60s and 70s tunes just loud enough for all to hear. It was a peaceful moment.

"Okay, so now that we have names for the boys, we should name the girls after famous singers we listen to. Not sure if you remember, but I used to sing *Silver Springs* by Fleetwood Mac when you were just a baby to get you to sleep. It never worked. How about we name the dark-haired pig Fleetwood? She seems chill. I like her soulful eyes," Mel suggested.

"I don't remember the song or you singing, but I like that name. Fleetwood. Put that song on next, Mel," Lennon answered.

"And the littlest of them all should be Joni after Joni Mitchell. She is no more than 25 pounds. Her salt and pepper hair is so smooth. She was so gentle when I picked her up and put her into the trailer. *Blue* is one of my favorite albums." Mel hummed the song *A Case of You*.

When they arrived at the ranch, Mel put the female pigs in one stall and the male pigs in the adjacent stall. Lennon filled up their water tanks and dropped pig pellets into six bowls. Lennon told each pig that they were safe and protected when she gave them their dinner. Mojo tried to share in their dinner, but was chased out of the stall several times.

"Hey, here you go, Joni. Have some more pellets." Lennon fed Joni extra food.

Mel connected her phone to the blue tooth speaker they kept in the barn and turned on some music.

"This big one over here is definitely pregnant. She is moving slowly. How about Joplin? Janis was such a vibe." Mel put on *Bobby McGee* and danced as the moon came up. Lennon danced too.

"Nina Simone for the last one. One of the best jazz singers of all time," Mel said as she sang *Feeling Good*.

"I love it," Lennon responded.

They danced and watched the pigs settle in until it was dark. And then it was time for everyone to go to bed.

The next morning, Mel, Lennon, and Mojo went to their local smoothie spot in Malibu to order some breakfast. As Mel watched the crowd place their orders, she had an idea and called the manager over.

"Hey, Morgan. We just rescued six pigs. I was wondering if you would let me use the fruits and vegetables from the day that you'd otherwise compost. The pigs would love it," Mel asked.

"Absolutely. Pigs are my favorite. And we always love supporting local businesses. I'll set aside a bag of produce for you to pick up. But for now, take this bag here. It has been a hectic morning. Malibu is certainly on a juice cleanse." Morgan handed over a large bag of fruits and veggies that would have otherwise been composted.

"Awesome. And as always, your team is always welcome to visit the farm and meet our new residents. See ya tomorrow." Mel walked out of the store with a massive bag of produce and a large smoothie.

Mel pulled into the ranch and drove to the barn. The pigs were in the stall. Mel opened the door for them to get some air. That morning, Slick had set up small animal fencing so the pigs could spend time outside, rooting. The fencing would be taken down once they were all placed, but it was safe enough for them to spend a few hours outside each day. There was mulch spread out for the pigs to root. A covered area that provided shade with water spritzers running kept the animals cool. The pigs were exploring. Lennon began lining up six bowls of food with pellets and produce. The pigs dashed over, and Lennon couldn't feed them fast enough. When they were done, she hand-fed them apples while Mel called the vet to schedule an onsite visit. The vet happened to be nearby and said she'd come over.

"Hey, Len. How awesome is all this produce from Sun Smoothies? I asked Morgan if they would donate their compost to us to eliminate waste, but also to help us cover the costs of providing these guys with proper nutrition. Community involvement and support are so cool. Locals helping locals to do more. You get it?" Mel asked.

"Awesome. Look, an apple, strawberries, banana, kale. A lot of kale. Why so much kale! I know that it is good to ask for help when you need it. And also to help when others need it," Lennon responded.

"It is a good lesson. It is a sign of strength to be comfortable asking for help," Mel said.

The vet finally arrived and began inspecting the pigs. "Looks like you got your hands full. Overall, their health is great. However, three of the female pigs are pregnant. I can't tell how many babies are in each belly. But Joplin here is about to give birth any day now. Nina would be next in line. Then Joni. Yes, little Joni is also pregnant. Fleetwood is the only one that is not pregnant," the vet explained.

"Wait. What? We thought Fleetwood was the only one that was pregnant. We got that all wrong! So, this changes things quickly. We need to figure out a plan as Joplin can't give birth at the ranch. I'm just not comfortable with piglets exploring this area as there are too many predators at night. Just last week, a family of coyotes crossed the property. I'll reach out to rescues in NorCal. We need to move as fast as possible to find a forever home as we are not equipped to be a forever home to these pigs and all their babies. One day, but not today," Mel responded.

Over the next few days, Mel networked the pigs into various rescues throughout California. Joplin was the first placement. Shortly after she arrived in Petaluma, California, she gave birth to seven piglets. All the piglets were healthy and continued living together with their mamma. Once a week, the piglets were taken to a Nursing Home where the patients could pet them on their laps. They brought a tremendous amount of joy to everyone there.

Fleetwood was the subsequent placement. She landed at a rescue in Southern California, located on a Native American Indian reservation. The air was sweet and warm, the night sky was magical, and energy ignited the land, making the atmosphere feel spiritually charged. Fleetwood continued to root in a large pasture with another pig who became her best friend.

Nina Simone ended up at Olivia's with the alpacas, Charles Bukowski and Allen Ginsberg. Nina gave birth to four beautiful, healthy piglets. They all lived in a pasture with other rescued pigs, sheep, and goats.

John Denver and Jim Morrison were placed together in Half Moon Bay, California. They became brand ambassadors to the rescue and were on the cover of their yearly magazine.

Two months later, after all the placements, all that was left was little pregnant Joni, who wasn't so little anymore. She grew much wider but still remained small. Mel and Lennon developed a very special bond with her. Because of her size, it was hard to tell how far along she was in the pregnancy. The vet came up for checks and was convinced she had a few more weeks to go.

One morning, after the horses were fed, Mel and Lennon went to check on little Joni. But when they got to the barn, Joni was nowhere in sight, which was odd as Joni always greeted people with a wagging tail. Mel ran into the stall and began sifting through the hay with her hands. Under a pile of hay in the corner, there was Joni in labor.

Mel called out to Lennon, "Lennon, Joni is going to have a baby. She can't have the baby here. I need your help quick. Grab some food. I'll carry her to our house so she can give birth comfortably."

Mel brought Joni into their den and made a nice comfortable space with water and a blanket. They then left her to do what she needed to do for a successful birth. They waited. And waited. And waited. And suddenly, Lennon shouted, "A piglet."

Mel came running over, and tottering around the den was the tiniest piglet they ever saw. The piglet fit into the palm of Mel's hand. Her eyes weren't open yet, and her skin was soft. She had almost no hair. And through her snout, she was making the most gentle noises. She explored but never roamed far from her mamma. Mel used Mojo's old exercise pen to set up an enclosure around Joni and her baby once she saw how mobile the baby was. She didn't want the piglet to get stuck under the couch. "Lennon, it's so cool that piglets can walk when they are born. I had to wait almost a year before you took your first steps. Let's go into the kitchen, where we can watch them from a distance. I don't want Joni to get nervous that we are close to her newborn. Moms can be protective. She may have more babies coming. It's rare that pigs only give birth to one," Mel said while she finished securing the exercise pen.

Lennon and Mojo stared from the kitchen. They couldn't believe that a piglet was in their house. Mojo was curious. All he wanted to do was lick and groom the piglet. Hours went by, they ate lunch, watching the two, and during dinner, Mel asked, "Hey, Lennon, it's supposed to be a full moon tonight. And not just any full moon; it's the Harvest Moon. This one shines the brightest, so we should keep our eyes open for it when the sun fully sets. The Harvest Moon represents abundance. The abundance of love, community, and even moonlight. What if we named the piglet Harvest? She has given us an abundance of joy. It is also one of Neil Young's best albums. Harvest Moon. This completes the set."

"Joni and Harvest. Mommy and daughter." Lennon loved it.

Lennon and Mojo were getting sleepy and went to bed. Whereas Mel went to check on Joni and Harvest to ensure they were both doing well. She brought water, cantaloupe and watermelon. Harvest was latching and drinking milk from Joni. They were bonding. Mel thought it was odd that Joni was now recovering with only one piglet. She began searching the blanket and found what she had suspected was a stillborn piglet. "Oh, Joni, I am so sorry. You gave birth to a second baby, and, unfortunately, that one didn't make it. Your body has been through so much. Rest up." Mel began petting Joni to comfort her. Mel and Joni stayed in that moment to acknowledge the loss of her baby. Mel then removed the stillborn, wrapped her in a towel, and planned on burying her on the ranch.

Mel stayed up all night with Joni, listening to the Harvest Moon album. She was nervous that Joni would accidentally roll over onto Harvest. Early the next day, Mel made a large pot of coffee. Lennon and Mojo came running into the den, very well-rested. Unlike Mel.

"Mom, are they okay? Did she have more babies?" Lennon asked.

"Both Joni and Harvest are doing great. Joni did give birth to another baby. Unfortunately, she passed away before being born. Which means she gave birth to a stillborn. Things like this happen to humans and animals alike. We must trust that it was what Mother Nature intended," Mel said.

Lennon processed that information and walked over to Joni. "I'm sorry, Joni. Here, take my Lovey Bear. Lovey Bear comforts me when I feel sad. You have Harvest. Harvest is so cute," she said and hugged her. That entire day was spent in the den, hanging out. Harvest hopped around while Joni rested. Mojo watched with delight and shared Joni's watermelon snack. Their nighttime looked the same, eating and resting. It was time for bed, and Lennon asked if she and Mojo could sleep in the living room with the pigs. Mel agreed because this was such a rare occasion, and everyone had an indoor campout.

The next day, Mel began making calls to rescues in San Diego to find the two a home. One of her trusted contacts suggested reaching out to a woman who fostered pigs for their rescue in the past. She seemed credible, so Mel gave her a call. Mel and Jennifer spoke, and there was an instant connection. She agreed to foster Joni and Harvest until a forever home was secured. This was excellent as Mel couldn't keep a pig in her house much longer. Lennon disagreed but went along with the plan.

A few days later, Mel, Lennon, and Mojo drove Joni and Harvest to their new home. Mel decided not to rush their transport as she wanted to ensure Harvest and Joni were strong. Harvest had put on several pounds and had become a chunky little thing. However, Joni's energy was restored, and she returned to her happy self.

"Mom, I know we can't keep the pigs, but I had the best time watching Harvest. I'll always remember this," Lennon said.

"Me too, Len. It was a wonderful experience. I think Joni will remember us too. We were there for the birth of her only daughter," Mel said.

"Like us?" Lennon asked

"Exactly like us," Mel said.

When they arrived, Jennifer and her husband were waiting outside. Their property was charming. It was fenced in with plenty of land for the pigs to run and root. A vegetable garden and a door connected the inside and out for the pigs to come and go as they pleased. There were enrichment toys on the ground, such as to treat balls and back scratchers. Jennifer carried Joni out of the truck and into her new room. Mel carried Harvest. Once they were all inside, Mel put Harvest on the floor. Jennifer began to cry as she was so excited and couldn't get over how cute she was. Her husband brought some food in, and they all watched them settle into their new fluffy bed. Shortly after that, Mel, Lennon, and Mojo said their goodbyes.

***

Christmas was soon in full swing. Mel and Lennon were at the feedstore, buying gifts for the horses and Ollie when Mel received a text. It was a picture of Harvest and Joni under Jennifer's Christmas tree. Mel showed Lennon, and they called Jennifer right away.

"That is the cutest picture ever. Harvest is wearing a Santa hat. And Joni is wearing a mistletoe crown. Incredible. How is it going?" Mel asked.

"I'm glad you called. I wanted to talk to you. I know you've been trying to find a forever home. We would like to be that to Joni and Harvest. They are part of our family, and I don't think we could part with them. They're eating asparagus in the yard at this very moment. I don't know the protocols, but may we keep the two?" Jennifer said.

"This is the best news. I was secretly hoping they would end up with you. You've taken such exceptional care of them. Yes, of course. They are yours. Can we come and visit, though?" Mel asked.

"Yes. Thank you. We are in love," Jennifer said, and they hung up the phones.

"Well, Len, we did it. Joni and Harvest are going to stay with Jennifer and Darren. We rescued all six pigs and the babies, and everyone's living very happy and peaceful lives. I'm proud of us. Thank you for encouraging me to do this rescue. When we choose kindness, we limit the suffering of others. We changed the lives of six pigs and so so many piglets." Mel laughed.

"We must always help the animals. And choose love. You know, I love ice cream. Let's get some." Lennon smiled.

"Sounds good, Len. Then we can head home and spend the afternoon with our boys,"

Mel said as she put her arm around Lennon's shoulders, and all three walked off.

CHAPTER ~6~

Found

It was a Friday morning, and Mel was driving Lennon to school. As they cruised down the Pacific Coast Highway, the sun came up over the ocean and its rays beamed into their truck. The windows were open, and Led Zeppelin played on the radio. Mojo stuck his head out of the sunroof and opened his mouth to taste the air. His lips flapping in the wind made a funny noise. Lennon had her sunglasses on upside down, and she declared herself to be on dolphin patrol. In the morning, the dolphins played close to the shore. Every so often, Mel heard Lennon shout, "I spy a dolphin. That's one. I spy a dolphin. That's two," she said each time they breached the ocean.

There were surfers catching waves, seagulls sunbathing on the sand, and large pelicans diving beak first into the Pacific Ocean, looking for some breakfast. On the other side of the highway, there were rolling green mountains filled with palm trees and boulders with homes tucked away in the hills. Conversations were limited as they jammed to the music and appreciated their beautiful surroundings. They were all feeling grateful for such a glorious morning.

When they arrived at school, Lennon hopped out of the truck and grabbed her backpack. Mel walked her to the big red door and told her she'd be there to pick her up at the end of the day. Lennon was met by her friends and her favorite teacher, and they all walked in together. As Mel waved goodbye, her phone rang.

"Hey, Mel. Thank you for picking up the phone. It's Maryanne. I know it's been so long since we spoke. I have something going on and really need your help," Maryanne stated.

"It is wonderful to hear from you. How can I help?" Mel replied.

"My dear friend's brother passed away a few days ago from health complications. He was at home with his dog by his side when it happened. The two were found next to each other, after a co-worker came over to the house to check in on him. His co-worker was concerned after he hadn't shown up for work in two days. Sometimes he drove her brother home. Not knowing a phone number or name of a family member, he decided to call the police. The police then located Gabby, his sister, and told her of the news. The sister is my good friend and, from what I know, the family wasn't close. It's been years since they have spoken. The police put the dog in his owner's gated backyard. There have been several robberies in the neighborhood, and maybe the cop thought the dog would keep the house safe until the family arrived. I'm calling you as I need help finding this dog a home. I don't know how many days he has been outside or if he has access to clean water and food. My guess is two days max." Maryanne cried.

"Oh, Maryanne. I am so sorry. That is such a sad story. Would you mind connecting me with a family member so I can make arrangements to meet the dog?" Mel replied.

"Gabby, his sister, is there all day today. I'll tell her you are coming by. She isn't on her phone much right now. I think she is just processing the death of her brother. I told her that I would coordinate," Maryanne said.

"Would Gabby want to adopt the dog? After all, it was her brother's," Mel asked.

"Gabby is unable to take the dog because she has two of her own and can't afford a third. I need you to prepare yourself; her brother had an array of mental health issues, one of which was being a hoarder. I am not sure about the condition of the home. Let me know what happens when you get there," Maryanne answered.

They hung up the phone, and Mel and Mojo drove to the dog store to pick up food, a leash, treats, bowls, and a large animal carrier. She then called her veterinarian to set up an appointment for the dog once they picked him up. They agreed to hold a spot open that afternoon. With time to spare, Mel and Mojo fed the horses and Ollie their lunch before picking Lennon up at school.

"Hey, Mojo. I sometimes struggle to decide whether or not I should bring Lennon on rescues such as these. I know this house will be in terrible condition. I think, as her parent, do I protect her and make sure that she only sees the beauty in the world? Or do I expose her to real life? Real-life includes sadness, pain, and circumstances that are not always perfect. I know she's young, but I also believe that she can handle the truth. In fact, I think she does better knowing the truth. The more she experiences acts of kindness and compassion, the more those words will mean something to her as she lives within that value system. Kindness and compassion for animals transcend to people and the environment too. Compassion is not limited and neither is love. These are expansive ideologies. I'm going to bring her along with us. Oh Mojo, I love when you look so deeply into my eyes when we talk. You are so soulful, my angel boy," Mel said while petting Mojo.

When Mel pulled up to school, Lennon came charging out of the big red door. "What's going on, Mom? Hi, Mojo," Lennon shouted and hugged him.

"Hey, Lennon. How was school?" Mel asked.

"It was good. Let's get some ice cream," Lennon suggested.

They drove to their favorite ice cream parlor in Venice Beach and ordered two cones with extra sprinkles. They walked to a bench to sit down and eat.

Mel began talking. "Hey, Lennon. I got a call this morning about a dog that needs our help. So I thought we'd go check it out after our ice cream."

"What happened to the dog?" Lennon asked.

"Well, his owner passed away from a variety of health issues. The dog needs a home as no other family member can take him. My concern is that if we don't help now, there is a chance this dog could end up at a shelter. The shelters don't need any more dogs. They are already at capacity," Mel said.

"What's the dog's name?" Lennon asked.

"As far as I know, the dog doesn't have a name. I mean, he does, but no one seems to know it. From what I understand, the man that passed away didn't keep in touch with his family. His one friend who found them didn't know the dog's name either. Maybe the owner was a very private person. I'm not here to judge the depth of any of these relationships. Life is complicated. We were called to find this dog a great home. And that is exactly what we are going to do," Mel said.

"That is really, really sad. He must've had a name, but no one knows it. He needs a great name, for he is a great dog. I know it. He is a boy, right?" Lennon asked.

"Yes. That is all we know—another thing I wanted to talk to you about. The owner had a mental illness. He was a hoarder," Mel said.

"What's a hoarder?" Lennon interrupted.

"Well, a hoarder collects things. A lot of things. It can be anything, really. And these collections grow and, in some cases, take over the house and property. A hoarder has a hard time letting go," Mel answered.

"Was I a hoarder with my fruit collections?" Lennon asked.

"No. The biggest lesson we learned was understanding separation. And being okay when it was time to discard or compost your fruit," Mel responded.

"So there will be a lot of stuff everywhere?" Lennon asked.

"Most likely. And I like to play it safe. So I'll have you and Mojo wait in the truck like you did when we rescued A Pig Named Love," Mel answered.

Lennon sucked the ice cream out of the bottom of her cone, finished the last bite, wiped her hands off and said, "I understand. Let's go rescue this dog."

When they pulled up to the house, it was even worse than Mel expected. The house windows were boarded up with plywood. Two old rusted cars were parked on the lawn with tires blown out.

Broken sporting equipment filled the front and back seats with oversized stuffed animals thrown in. Plants and vines were growing out of the car windows. There were food wrappers and plastic bottles on the walk up to the front door. The trees hadn't been trimmed, and large, heavy branches rested on the roof, creating a constant shade of darkness hanging over the home. A small woman appeared from the side entrance, wearing gloves and a mask.

Mel got out of her truck. "Are you Gabby?"

"Yes, Mel?" Gabby responded.

"Yup. Maryanne gave us your address and said we could come by this afternoon to meet the dog," Mel replied.

"Of course. I am so happy to see you," Gabby said.

"I brought my kid and my dog with me. I will leave them in the car," Mel said as she began unloading the leash and some dog food.

Gabby agreed.

"I'll be right back. If you need anything, just yell," Mel said to Lennon and Mojo.

"You got it," Lennon responded as she climbed into the front seat, rolled down the window, and looked at the property.

"I'm really sorry for your loss. Just know we will do everything we can to make sure this dog gets placed into a good home," Mel commented as they walked to the back gate.

"I know. Maryanne is a good friend of mine. She spoke so highly of you. I trust you guys. The dog is really sweet. I gave him some clean water when I got here this morning," Gabby responded.

Mel heard a howling in the distance. When she got to the backyard gate, there was the dog. He was pushing his nose through metal poles, wagging his tail quickly. The howls were a way for him to communicate that he was there and wanted to be found. He was so excited that they responded. Mel first noticed his eyes. They were light brown, soft, and gentle. He was a husky mix. His coat was white, brown, and grey. His ears were pointed. He weighed about 50 pounds. His fur made him appear bigger. Mel opened the gate and bent down to give him some food. She emptied the first can into a bowl, and the dog devoured it. So she gave him more food, and he devoured that as well. When he finished both food bowls, Mel began to pet his head. He leaned into her with his entire body for scratches. He knew human attention by the way he was receiving Mel's loving pets. It was so clear that his owner loved him too. Mel took a look around the backyard to see if any other animals were trapped or needed help. Hoarding wasn't just limited to stuff. People could hoard animals too.

There were broken bicycles, a washer, and dryer, a refrigerator, woodpiles, metal poles, and crutches. A purple beanbag soaked with water and leaves sat in the middle of a path, attracting bugs. There was a yellow shed in the corner of the yard that looked weathered. Mel peeked through its window and saw dusty chairs, broken bookshelves, torn cushions from a couch, a record player, and cardboard boxes of baseball cards, records, magazines, etc. Mel tried to push the door open, but it was jammed shut. Wires and tubes from heavy machinery were all over the backyard. There were sneakers, clothes, and trash everywhere. Mel looked at Gabby. "I am going to take the dog with me. I'll take him directly to the vet. He won't be able to handle another night of rain and cold without proper shelter."

"I trust your judgement," Gabby answered and began to cry. "I am so embarrassed that you had to see my brother's home. But, I am grateful that you're going to take the dog. I've been worried about him most. I have dogs of my own. My heart breaks; you guys have given me hope and some light."

"Please don't be embarrassed. Life is really hard. The only thing we can do is be kind to one another. Your brother was kind to this dog. We work in animal rescue. I have seen what hate and neglect look like and the damage they can cause to animals. A dog that has suffered from neglect or abuse doesn't lean into belly rubs and back scratches like this dog. They would hide in a corner, growl, bark, shake and fear all human contact. They could even get skittish and run away from their rescuer. I hold a space in my heart for your brother. I promise that I'll find his dog a wonderful home," Mel said and hugged Gabby.

Mel gently put a slip leash around the dog's neck. "Let's go, buddy," Mel reassured him that he was safe as they left the backyard. Lennon spotted them. "Mom, you got him," she said and jumped out of the truck with Mojo. Lennon was very used to having calm energy around new rescues. She learned the difference between loud energy and calm energy from being around the horses at Moonlight Mile Ranch. Loud energy is yelling, which could make the animal nervous or reactive. But if you remain calm and breathe slowly, the animal will feel safe, protected and trusting of their human. They will have confidence in people as leaders.

"We did, Lennon. Be careful. I still don't know his personality, but he is kind and loving so far. Get Mojo's leash on, and let's walk to the corner. Stay behind me, though," Mel said.

They all walked to the corner. The dog was happily smelling the trees, Mojo, and fire hydrants. Mel decided that the crate was unnecessary for transport, and he'd be fine in the truck with them.

When they got in the truck, Lennon noticed a horrendous smell coming from the dog. He smelled of mildew, dirt, and outside. Laughing and holding her breath, Mel rolled down the windows. The dog stuck his head out and smiled at the sun. It was as if he knew that a new life had begun. Mojo did the same thing in the front seat. And soon, they both had their heads out of the sunroof.

"Mom, what will we name him?" Lennon said.

"Not sure. What are you thinking?" Mel asked.

"Jude," Lennon responded.

"How do you figure Jude?" Mel asked.

"We were listening to *Hey Jude* on the way here, and one line is, take a sad song and make it better," Lennon responded.

"Go on," Mel said

"Well, it's simple. The song is about taking a sad or bad situation and making it better, which is what we are trying to do with Jude right now. The Beatles also taught us that Love Is All You Need. Jude is a cool name. Jude, do you want to wear my sunglasses?" Lennon smiled.

"Jude, do you like your new name?" Mel asked. Jude brought his head back into the truck and licked Lennon. "Jude, you sure are cool. Lennon was right."

When they arrived at the vet, a technician greeted them. "We've been waiting for you guys. And who might our new patient be?"

"Jude. He smells," Lennon shouted.

"Oh boy. What a great name. The doctor will call you once we're done. Come on, let's get you checked out," the technician said and walked Jude inside.

It was nearly dark now, and the three were hungry for dinner. They drove to their local taco spot, ordered at the counter, and sat down.

"What an amazing day," Mel commented.

"Jude is really awesome. How are we going to find him a home? Can he stay with us?" Lennon asked.

"I'd love to have Jude be part of our family, but not every animal we save is meant to be ours. I'll call Amy and Sherman to see if they know anyone that would foster him until he finds a forever home. They both have placed so many dogs into great homes. The good news is we get a sleepover with him tonight," Mel said as the food arrived.

Mel called Amy and Sherman. They agreed to reach out to their network. Amy came back first with a lead. Amy was able to locate a young man that had a successful history of fostering cats. He agreed to foster Jude as, two weeks before, he babysat for a husky puppy while his best friend traveled for work and fell in love with the breed. He understood the needs of these dogs in terms of hikes, food, and play time. It was arranged that Jude would be dropped off at his foster home tomorrow as it was getting late.

The vet's office called. "We have wonderful news. Jude is in perfect health. We bathed him. He was really smelly and needed some hydration. Everyone is in love with him. He's ready for pick-up," the technician said.

When they arrived at the vet, Jude was outside on a walk. Lennon ran over and hugged Jude. Jude was so excited to see Lennon that he started to lick her face. Then Mojo came over, and they began to play. After they greeted each other, they all got into the truck and returned to their ranch for a sleepover.

At the house, Jude followed Mojo around. The first stop was the dog bed and water bowl. Next, he sniffed the dog toys and inspected a bone. Next, he was curious about the rest of the space, so he walked into Lennon's room, then Mel's room. Finally, when he felt it was safe and comfortable, he jumped up on the couch and settled in. Mel could tell he was excited and tired at the same time.

"Lennon, I think Jude will sleep well tonight. He's had such a long few days," Mel said.

"I'll watch one program with Jude before I sleep," Lennon said and jumped onto the couch next to him. Lennon snuggled up and said, "Mom, come look at Jude's eyes. He looks sad."

Mel walked over to the couch to check on Jude. "Lennon, you are correct. Jude does have a sad look in his eyes. Jude has been through a lot these past few days. He finally feels safe to emote and has feelings of sadness and pain. Remember when Joni lost her baby? This is a similar feeling of loss and sadness," Mel explained while petting Jude's head.

Lennon started to kiss Jude's nose. "I am sorry, Jude. I am sorry that your owner died. He loved you. And you loved him too. It is okay to have feelings. Sometimes when I'm sad, I hold my Lovey Bear close. Here, Lovey will comfort you too."

Mojo got close to Jude and began licking his head. Grooming is a way for dogs to express their affection toward one another. Mel watched the two of them comfort Jude. They were both doing such a wonderful job, being there for him and letting him feel sadness and pain. They didn't force him to play, nor did they dismiss what he was feeling. They just gave him an emotionally safe space to be.

Lennon started to close her eyes and retired to her room to go to sleep. Mojo and Jude followed Lennon and jumped onto her bed. Lennon covered the dogs with her blanket and gave Jude and Mojo a kiss goodnight. Later on, Mel came in to check on everyone. Mojo, Jude, and Lennon were all in bed, cuddling. Lennon was between the two boys with her hands above her head. The dogs were in the same position with their paws. Mel closed the door, leaving it cracked open for the boys to leave if they wanted. Then, Mel went to sleep in her room.

The next morning, Mel was awakened by Lennon shouting from her bedroom, "It's Saturday morning. No school for me. Jude. Mojo. Wake up. Let's go get Mom. I want pancakes." There was a stampede down the hallway. Then Lennon and the dogs jumped onto the bed where Mel was lying awake. "Get up," Lennon shouted. Lennon walked out of the room with Jude right next to her and began showing him her toys and books. Lennon drew a picture of Jude. They listened to her favorite John Denver album and danced to *Take Me Home, Country Roads*. During breakfast, Lennon read Jude a book about love.

"Mom, Jude doesn't have a collar. He's been naked since we got him. Can we go to the dog store and get him a collar before dropping him off? He should be dressed when he meets his new daddy," Lennon asked.

"Wonderful idea, Len. You can pick it out," Mel said.

It was time to leave and take Jude to his new home. They loaded up the truck, and everyone assumed their seats from yesterday. Mojo took the front seat, and Lennon and Jude shared the back seat. The windows were rolled down, the dogs stuck their heads out. They were on their way.

When they got to the dog store, Lennon picked out a red collar that read Found. She put it on him. "Jude, you are now dressed and looking handsome. Red is my favorite color. The color of love. It says Found. We found you, and you found love. When you miss me at your new home, just scratch the collar and know I am thinking about you too," Lennon said to Jude.

"Lennon, you know how we always say it's important to adopt an animal rather than shop for one? And we say that because there are so many animals at the shelters that need a home," Mel asked.

"Yes," Lennon answered.

"Well, it is also really important to understand how important it is to foster animals. Just like Jude's new foster dad is doing. He is a hero, too. Placing animals into people's homes until they are adopted allows rescue workers, like ourselves, to continue to save dogs, cats or any other animal for that matter, from hard situations. The act of fostering keeps the animals out of the shelters. Fostering is a beautiful act of selflessness. It is really important to acknowledge the work that goes into it," Mel explained.

"It is like we were fosters to the piggies before we found them forever homes. And because we acted as fosters, we could save them all," Lennon replied.

"Exactly," Mel said.

When they got to the foster's home, a tall young man with very bright sneakers stood outside.

"Guys, park over here. I saved this spot for you," the man called.

"Awesome. I'm Mel. This is Lennon, Mojo, and Jude," Mel said and they all got out of the truck.

"Wow! Jude is so handsome. He is even cooler than the pictures Amy sent to me. Jude, I'm Jay. I am your new foster dad. I am so excited to meet you," Jay said while petting and kissing Jude.

"He likes you, Jay. Do you have any questions before we head out?" Mel asked.

"Nah. I babysat a Husky puppy. I am so ready for this. I got all kinds of food for you, Jude," Jay said with a smile.

"Jude. You are magical. I am so grateful that I had the chance to meet you." Mel kissed Jude on the nose goodbye.

"Jude. Remember your red collar. I am always with you." Lennon kissed Jude on the head.

Mojo and Jude played for a bit longer, and then Mojo jumped into the truck.

Later that evening, Mel received a video text message from Jay. "Hey, Lennon, come here. Let's watch this video of Jude together," Mel said.

The video showed Jude sitting on the couch, howling at the evening sky. Jude sounded like a wolf calling out for his pack. "He may miss us, Lennon."

The foster commented, "A nice quiet evening in with my new friend." They watched the video over and over. Jude was smiling.

The following morning, they woke up to another video text message. It was Jude, sitting on the Hollywood Walk of Fame with Jay. Jay was drinking a morning coffee while Jude was howling at all the cars driving by. Jude looked like a street performer, and everyone that walked by smiled at him. Jay commented, "Still howling."

"Mom, why does Jude howl so much?" Lennon asked.

"So many reasons. It could be a call to his pack, or he might be wanting attention, or maybe he found something for his owner to look at or a call for help. In this video, Jude is most likely chiming in with other street artists and sirens from passing cop cars," Mel responded.

Later on, another video text message came in. It was Jude, sitting in the back seat of a convertible sports car. He was looking all around with the wind in his hair. Fleetwood Mac's *"Gypsy"* played on their radio. It was a perfect Los Angeles scene. The only thing missing was a pair of sunglasses for Jude to wear. Jay commented, "On our way to the beach."

Mel sent a text back, "This is most likely Jude's first time at the beach. Amazing."

Lennon noted that Jude was still in his red collar. This made her happy.

The final video text message came in just after the sunset. It was Jude on the beach. He was chasing birds, cautiously running in the water, and playing with other dogs. His nose was sandy, and his legs were wet from the ocean. Jay commented, "I would like to adopt Jude. I want to be his forever home. He has touched my heart in a way that I didn't expect. We found each other, just like what his collar says, 'Found', which he loves. He won't let me take it off him. Red looks really good on him."

Lennon and Mojo were asleep when that message came in. Mel told Lennon the news over breakfast. Mel also let Maryanne and Gabby know that Jude found a forever home with his foster. It brought them both to tears. Mel went on to say that Jude was in perfect health. Despite her brother's mental illness, this dog was loved deeply. Everyone was thrilled with the news.

"So Lennon, another rescue complete. We found a beautiful dog and a wonderful home. What should we do today?" Mel said.

"I think we should spend the afternoon with the horses feeding them treats under the oak tree," Lennon suggested.

"Now that is a plan I like. Let's grab some apples from the refrigerator and head down to their pasture," Mel said. And the three of them walked out the house together.

CHAPTER ~7~

Norman

It was spring at Moonlight Mile Ranch. Wild purple flowers covered the mountainside. June's garden was blooming with strawberries that the desert cottontails noshed on throughout the day. Mel, Lennon, and Mojo were out in the pasture, mucking and grooming the horses, when a call came in from a California area code. Mel picked up. "This is Mel."

"Hi, Mel. My name is Tracy. I work on a dairy farm. I got your number from an animal sanctuary in Half Moon Bay, California. They reached out to me last year hoping we would surrender a male calf to them, which we did. I was looking to do the same again this year, but they said they had no more room for another animal. They recommended that I reach out to you," Tracy said.

"Hi, Tracy. Where is your farm located?" Mel answered.

"About an hour north of Napa. We have sixty Jersey cows, and all of them are pregnant going into calving season. I expect some of our cows to begin to give birth within the next week. Was wondering if you had space to take a male calf. There are always so many, and the farm has no use for them," Tracy explained.

"Yes, I'll take a calf," Mel said and paused to think about what Tracy said about having no use for an animal and discarding life so easily. Mel was familiar with the idea that there is no humane dairy but hearing Tracy's words hurt even more. Nevertheless, Mel knew she had to help this calf, and this was most likely the last call Tracy would make in order to find an unwanted calf a home. "Do the farm owners know that you're looking to release one of your animals to me?" Mel asked.

"Yes, they do. And they are fine. As long as it's male, they don't care. We need the females to keep producing milk for our dairy business. Last year, when we gave a calf to the sanctuary, they sent me updates on how he was doing. I loved seeing the progress and his new life. I want to be able to do that again this year. It felt really good. I am hoping we can rescue more cows in the future," Tracy replied.

"Will the calf have access to his mother's colostrum? Immediately receiving colostrum from his mother will provide the necessary antibodies to prevent sickness and disease. This will increase the calf's chance of survival. If you want to do a good thing, then providing access to vital nutrients is part of that success story," Mel asked.

"It depends on how quickly they are separated from their mothers. I'll do my best. Historically speaking, male calves will not receive any colostrum. This is a business, and we need to think about the most efficient methods," Tracy answered.

"Morally, I don't understand your business at all. I believe in allowing all animals to live with dignity and security, without having to produce anything in return," Mel said.

"Yeah, I am starting to understand that. I'll give you a call within the week," Tracy said, and they hung up their phones.

"Are we bringing a cow to Moonlight Mile?" Lennon asked.

"We sure are. Hey, have you seen Slick and June? I want to tell them about this news," Mel asked.

"They're in the garden. Follow me. You know, Mom, we never rescued a cow before. We have horses, a donkey that thinks he is a horse, and some of June's chickens," Lennon said.

When they arrived at the garden, Mel said, "Well, we got a call from a dairy farm in Northern California. They asked if we wanted a male calf, and I said yes. So I will bring the newborn back to Moonlight Mile as our barn is finally set up. Ultimately, we'll need to find this cow a forever home. But while he is with us, I want to make sure this calf is cozy and comfortable. Slick, can you lay a few bales of fresh straw on the floor to keep him warm at night?" Mel asked while eating one of June's strawberries.

"Absolutely. Really looking forward to putting our barn to use." Slick smiled.

That night, while Mel was tucking in Lennon, Lennon asked, "Why does the calf have to be male? Doesn't milk come from all cows?" Lennon asked.

"Well, no. To produce milk, a cow must be pregnant. And who can get pregnant? Females. No animal, including humans, can physically produce milk without being pregnant. So dairy farms, big and small, will impregnate a female cow over and over and over again. Female cows keep their business going. It's a long, painful, and sad life for the animal. But that is how we get milk, cheese, and other dairy products," Mel explained.

"So if there are only pregnant cows giving us milk, what happens to the males?" Lennon asked.

"Male calves are sold for their meat, which is called veal. That's why it's important we help this cow. It is so rare that a dairy farm surrenders a calf, so when they do, it's important for sanctuaries to be there for the animal," Mel said.

Lennon took an intense breath and hugged Mojo, who was already sleeping and snoring on the pillow next to hers.

"You know who would love to meet a cow? Sherman." Lennon smiled.

"I bet. I was planning on asking her to take the trip up north with us to pick him up. She has experience with baby animals. Think she fostered newborn kittens, one of the harder animals to bottle feed. That's a skill that would really come in handy," Mel responded.

"Totally. Good night, Mom," Lennon said and turned over to go to sleep.

The next morning, Mel got out of bed to make coffee and call Sherman. The only question Sherman had for Mel was, "Is that kid coming too?" The answer was yes. Mel ordered powdered calf formula and bottles that she would pick up at the feed store later that day. She then rented a minivan, knowing there wouldn't be enough room in her truck for two adults, a child, a dog, and a calf to fit comfortably. Having seats that could fold down was necessary so the calf could stretch and stand if he was strong enough. Tracy called and confirmed that three females were hours away from going into labor and suggested that their team leave that evening as one would most likely be a male. The plan was set. Before Lennon fell asleep, they'd get into the minivan and head out.

Sherman was a perfect partner for rescue such as this. Given that her personality ran anxious, she effortlessly stayed up, talking with Mel as they drove throughout the night. Sherman offered to share the driving, but when she got behind the wheel, she looked in her bag and realized she had left her driving glasses at home. Sherman was one of the most responsible people Mel knew; leaving things at home was not something Sherman did. Sherman just doesn't like to drive, especially at night. She caught Mel up on the rescue dogs, "I have never seen so many fleas and ticks in my life.

I've been doing this animal business for a very long time. Hank and Seymour were covered. I groomed them twice. Afterwards, they looked fantastic, like movie stars. What on earth were they thinking! After a few weeks at my house, with consistent love and security, they settled in with the rest of my dogs and ended up bonding with my goats." Mel caught Sherman up on the alpacas, Charles Bukowski and Allen Ginsberg.

Night transitioned into the day. The sun beamed into the minivan's windows, waking Lennon and Mojo up. Sherman finished her last roll of Starburst. Mel sipped coffee that was sitting in the cup holder overnight.

"Alright, we are minutes away from the property. Let's stretch, go to the bathroom and prepare a bottle for the calf. Then, I'll send Tracy a text," Mel said.

"I have everything ready and will fold the seats down so there's room. I'm so happy we rented this minivan," Sherman said.

"Good morning, Sherman." Lennon smiled as she walked around to the back of the minivan.

Mojo hopped out to pee on the nearest tree.

"Listen, Lennon. I'm going to be sitting in the back on the way home so I can feed and monitor the calf. I have no idea what to expect," Sherman said.

"I'll help you. Even though you don't love being near kids." Lennon smiled.

Mel knew there was a small part of Sherman that loved the attention from Lennon. Sherman would never admit it, but they had a special relationship. Sherman also knew how much Lennon cared for the animals, and she deeply respected those qualities.

"Let's rock'n'roll. Lennon and Mojo, you know the drill. Stay in the car while Sherman and I get the calf," Mel said.

When they arrived, Tracy was standing outside, waving. They pulled up next to her and introduced themselves.

"I'm Tracy. Good to finally meet you in person. Come this way, the little guy is right over here," Tracy said as she led them to a nearby stall.

Inside the stall, Mel and Sherman saw a small calf, smaller than Mojo, with soft brown fur and fuzzy ears. His eyes looked big and droopy. He lifted his head ever so slightly but was so weak.

"Where is his mother?" Mel asked. Tracy pointed to the field and said, "I'm so sorry."

"Me too," Mel responded.

It was clear that this calf never received colostrum from his mother. Sherman wasn't expecting anything different but was still furious and picked up the calf and walked to the minivan with him in her arms. Mel opened the trunk door and helped place him in a soft spot. Sherman got in after him and quickly fed him his first bottle.

Sherman held his head up and reassured him that he was safe in her arms. Once the calf finished the bottle, Mel bent down. "We're going to take you home. I thank your mother for having you, and I'm sending her healing light to let her know that you are safe," Mel said.

Mel got into the front seat. "Tracy, thank you for reaching out. I'm here to help for any future rescue," Mel said and then turned around to look at the team in the back seat, "Belts on! We're getting out of here."

"Please send me pictures and updates." Tracy waved goodbye.

Lennon buckled up. "Is the calf going to be okay?"

"Unfortunately, I don't have that answer. These next few hours are going to be critical. He has only been alive for a few hours and has been through so much." Mel said.

Mojo positioned himself towards the calf. He began grooming his face to let him know he would be okay and then rested his head down. Mojo had such calming energy around all the new animals.

About three hours in, the calf seemed to look more alert. He was picking his head up and looking around, as though he was present in his body. Mel pulled into a gas station to fill up. Sherman was exhausted. "Hey, Lennon. Switch seats with me. I need more candy if I want to make it back to the ranch," Sherman said as she got out of the car.

Mel pumped the gas while Lennon climbed into the back of the minivan and sat next to the calf. She began petting his head and body. The windows were cracked open, and Mel listened to Lennon. "You know, mister, I never met a cow before. Let alone a cow as beautiful as you. Did you know that you have white hair above your eyelid and around your black nose? Did you know that you are brown? That is Mom's favorite color. You're going to be all right, especially with my Mom and Sherman watching over you right now. They know what they're doing. It's a great feeling to know you are loved. I will make sure you know what love is,"

Sherman got back to the car with a bag of candy in her hand, peeked into the window, saw Lennon petting the calf, and walked around to see Mel. "She's fine, I guess. I got some candy for all of us to share," Sherman said.

"Lennon will love sharing candy with you," Mel responded.

At sunset, the minivan pulled into Moonlight Mile Ranch. Mel lifted the calf out of the minivan and into his new stall. They gathered around and watched as he took a few exploratory steps and then found himself a cozy corner. Mojo sniffed the straw and tried to play with the calf. Sherman unloaded the extra formula and stored it in the tack room.

"Sherman, thank you so much for your help. Do you want me to see if Slick can give you a ride home? You live so close to the ranch," Mel asked.

"Are you nuts! I'm not leaving you to do this on your own all night. Why don't you and that kid get us some blankets? We're all sleeping in here," Sherman pronounced.

Mel knew Sherman was right. The best plan was to have eyes on the calf and rotate the feeding every few hours.

On the walk to the house, Mel checked in with Lennon. "Lennon, how you are doing?" Mel asked.

"I'm tired from the trip but so excited to have a slumber party. I think his name should be Norman. He feels like a Norman to me," Lennon said.

"Norman it is." Mel responded.

Mel returned with blankets, chairs, and a camping cot for Lennon. Sherman wrapped herself in one of the blankets and took a seat in the chair. As they were all getting comfortable, Slick and June entered the stall.

"Hey guys, I made you some warm food. Figured ya'll would be exhausted and hungry," June said as she handed them all a plate.

"Mel, don't you worry about that mess in the minivan. I'll make sure it's all clean. Not sure I can do much about the cow smell. That'll be something you can work out with the rental company." Slick said.

"It will most definitely be an interesting conversation. June, this food is delicious. Who taught you how to make such a wonderful spaghetti dish?" Mel asked.

"It's my mother's recipe. According to her, all the ingredients need to be fresh. So I picked some from our garden," June responded.

"I've been eating candy for a day. Which is not so unusual for me, but this is delicious and just what I needed. Thank you, June. This means a lot to me," Sherman devoured her meal.

"So, Lennon, are you going to introduce us?" June asked.

"Norman, this is June and Slick. They are safe people. They live here at the ranch and help us run the place. They are like our second family," Lennon said while sitting next to the calf. "June, want me to show you how to prepare a bottle? I watched Sherman do it on our ride home."

"I would love that." June and Lennon walked to the tack room.

"Ladies, I am going to assume that neither of you will get great sleep in here tonight. So I'll take care of all the chores in the morning, and June will prepare breakfast and coffee. How is Norman doing?" Slick asked.

"He responded well to the formula. But still uncertain, and we can't be too comfortable yet," Sherman said.

"When we got him, he was lethargic. Now he looks better. I feel safe with him here and our team looking out for him. How were the horses today?" Mel said.

"You know, Hickory and Ollie misbehaved moderately at lunch. First, Ollie tried to kick Hickory in the chest. And then he nipped Peanut on the rear. That donkey thinks he's the biggest one in the pasture. They sure are a bonded herd." Slick smiled.

"The little ones always have the boldest personalities," Mel said.

"I knew that Ollie was special from day one. I'm still grateful that he is yours now," Sherman said.

Lennon and June came back into the stall, and Lennon showed June exactly how to give Norman his bottle. Finally, Norman stood up to drink. Once the bottle was finished, June and Slick closed the barn doors and walked back to their home for the evening.

As Lennon grew more and more tired, she asked Mel, "Is this what you had to do with me when I was a baby? Stay up all night?"

"Exactly what I did with you. For many, many, many nights," Mel responded.

"One of the many reasons I won't ever have a kid," Sherman chimed in.

They all laughed, and shortly after, Lennon fell asleep. Mel and Sherman rotated feeds every three hours, but neither slept well. Then, before they knew it, June knocked on the door.

"Morning. The vet just pulled in. I made some coffee, fruit, and oatmeal. Mojo, I brought you breakfast too." June placed the food down and let the vet into the stall.

"Well, what do we have here? A sleepover? I've never seen this before."

Dr. Howard smiled. Dr. Howard was a well-known bovine veterinarian in Malibu.

"Dr. Howard. This is Norman. So wonderful to see you," Mel noted.

Dr. Howard examined the little cow's body and drew some blood. "I'll run the blood so we can get a baseline. Then, keep feeding him formula every few hours and call with any changes."

"Sherman, head home. Slick will give you a ride. Lennon, time for us to go into the house and shower," Mel said.

"Sounds good." Sherman took a sip of coffee, stretched, and called for Slick.

Lennon kissed Norman on the head, and they walked back to the house.

When Mel went down for Norman's afternoon bottle, she noticed he had diarrhea and decided to call Dr. Howard as that was a new development. Dr. Howard suggested that Mel bring Norman into his office so his team could monitor him overnight.

June agreed to watch Lennon and Mojo while Mel took Norman to the vet who was only a twenty-minute car ride. The vet tech came out to greet Mel. "Dr. Howard will be in touch. Our team will give Norman extra love and attention. Get some sleep, Mel. You guys are doing great work and must be exhausted," the vet tech said.

A week later, Norman returned to Moonlight Mile Ranch. Dr. Howard noted that Norman's symptoms were common in calves that never received colostrum, and he treated them with electrolytes and antibiotics. Norman was excited to be back at the ranch. When he saw Mojo, he ran over and nudged Mojo's body. Then, Mojo began playing with Norman.

Lennon came running down the hill and gave Norman the biggest hug, "Norman! I missed you so much."

They were all very excited to see a healthy and happy calf. Mel opened Norman's stall doors that led to an enclosed pasture where Norman could graze. Over the next few weeks, Norman's health continued to improve.

"Hey, Lennon, I think it's time we had a conversation about Norman and his forever home. He's now at the point in his development where he needs to learn how to be a cow. And in order to do that, he needs other cows. We, you, did such a fantastic job saving his life and getting him strong. All the promises you made about knowing love you have made good on: Norman will always remember you and Moonlight Mile," Mel said.

"But Ollie never had a donkey friend," Lennon replied.

"True. Ollie came to us a little older than Norman. He learned how to be a donkey in the first few years of his life. While it wasn't in the best of conditions, he was born into a family and spent time with other donkeys. When he arrived at Moonlight Mile, he was old enough to bond with Hickory and Peanut. They taught him herd dynamics, connection, and leadership," Mel answered.

"I don't understand why we can't rescue another calf from that farm? We have land." Lennon responded.

"I know there are more calves that we could rescue. And saying no breaks my heart. I want to be able to save them all and limit the amount of suffering for these animals. But right now, we don't have the resources to raise cows. Slick and I would need to fence in a new pasture, run water pipes underground to have clean, fresh water, and then the medical. All this takes time and money. But, I promise this can be our next project so we can be a home to two very special cows one day. How does that sound?" Mel answered.

"Okay. So, what is the plan now?" Lennon asked.

"Well, I was in touch with a rescue near San Diego dedicated to rescuing cows. They have over fifteen acres of pasture to graze. They've been saving space for a newborn calf. I sent them pictures of Norman. Sammy, the owner, agreed to be Norman's forever home. In fact, there is another cow there, also rescued from a dairy farm, that's just a few months older than Norman. So they can grow up together and learn how to survive from the more mature herd," Mel said.

"I'm going to miss him. Remember when we had a slumber party. We never had a slumber party with Hickory," Lennon said.

That weekend, Mel, Lennon, Mojo, and Norman got into their truck and took a trip down to San Diego. Lennon sat next to Norman, resting his head on her lap. Norman was peaceful and curious at times. There were moments when Norman and Mojo both had their heads out the window, and passing cars slowed down to take pictures.

When they pulled up to the rescue, a large sign read, "Sammy's Sanctuary for Cows." Behind it, the cows were grazing and behind the cows was Sammy waving a hello from the middle of the pasture. Sammy came running over.

"We made it," Mel said as she got out of the truck.

Lennon opened the back seat. "I'm Lennon. This is Norman. Norman is very special to me. Norman is magic. There is no other word to describe him. So please, take really great care of him," Lennon said.

"On it, Captain. I promise to give him the best life he could ever know. I hope you'll come to visit him." Sammy lifted Norman out of the truck. Norman stood. Looked around. Took a breath and then let out a sigh. Sammy, Norman, Lennon, and Mojo walked to Norman's new stall. Mel lagged, taking in the moment, watching them all walk together. The friendship and bonds between a cow, a child and a dog were immeasurable.

CHAPTER ~8~

Chance Avocado

It was a Sunday afternoon. Slick, June and Lennon were pulling into Moonlight Mile Ranch after spending a day at the farmers market, selling their produce harvested at the ranch. As always, Lennon hopped out of the truck first and shouted, "We are back."

"How did it go today?" Mel asked.

"Best day yet. Our lettuce and tomatoes sold out. We have some cucumbers left, which I'm going to cut up and eat for a snack," June said.

"I sold one of my paintings to Sherman. It was Ollie's picture," she continued.

"I can't believe I'm buying art from a kid, but this is good, and it's Ollie," Lennon said in Sherman's voice.

"What are you going to do with your earnings?" Mel asked.

"I'm going to buy a cactus for my plant collection and art supplies for my business," Lennon responded.

"Wonderful." Mel smiled. "Slick, you are quiet. You good?"

"I'm hanging in. The sun wipes me out. I had a terrific lunch at this taco stand, I think it's called the Salsa Shack. Try it next time you go to the farmers market. But I spent most of my day watching June and Lennon sell their products to our local community," Slick said.

"Sounds like everyone had a great day. While all of you were out, I got a call from my friend Becky who lives in Oregon, about a horse located in Southern California that needs our help," Mel said.

"What's the story with the horse?" Lennon asked.

"Well, it's a complicated one. This couple was living in a house in San Bernardino," Mel said.

"Oh no! Not San Bernardino," Lennon interrupted.

"Yes, Lennon, San Bernardino again. I feel the same, though," Mel said. "Anyway, this couple left their home and all their belongings behind. We aren't concerned about material items, but they left behind a horse, some pigs, and chickens. We got the call to help the horse," Mel said.

"What about the pigs and chickens?" asked June.

"Lois, a good Samaritan, and a neighbor are there today to meet with the rescue taking the pigs and chickens. She's been staying on-site to make sure no one, who isn't supposed to, take the animals," Mel responded. "Our mission is getting this horse out."

"Seems straightforward. What is the complicated part?" asked Slick.

"Well, the horse has a difficult time walking. From the information I received, along with some pictures, this horse had incurred an injury on his front right hoof. He got it stuck in a barbed-wire fence, mangling the hoof and muscle tissue. He was never treated by a vet, so the hoof began growing backwards. The shape and length immediately tell me this injury has gone untreated for years. In addition, the other three hoofs are totally overgrown, making it difficult and painful to walk. This horse has learned to use his entire body to compensate for the pain in his legs," Mel said.

"Just terrible! Why have an animal if you don't want to care for them?" Slick said.

"Wait a minute! If the horse can't walk, how do we get him into the trailer?" Lennon asked.

"We try our best. Having a horse that can't or won't walk makes this rescue challenging. Once we are on-site and see him, we can assess the situation better. We need to go prepared. So, what does that mean? Calm energy, patience, and a ton of treats," Mel responded.

"Should I clear out the stall we used for Norman?" Slick asked.

"No. I spoke with our vet, and we agreed it was best to take him directly to the horse hospital for screening and bloodwork to see what is going on internally," Mel answered.

"Makes sense. So how can we help?" Slick asked.

"Once we unload the produce from the truck, we can attach the trailer with the ramp. This way, we can wake up and go," Mel said.

"Sure thing," June responded.

Later that evening, Lennon was getting into her bed. Mojo already took over one side of the bed and was snoring loudly, occasionally wagging his tail, making a thumping sound on the bed. "Mommy, do you think Mojo is dreaming of the beach?"

"The beach or pizza," Mel responded.

"He is funny. He eats everything. Can I come with you tomorrow?" Lennon asked.

"Of course, Lennon. I want you to be there with Mojo and me." Mel said.

"Good. I'm going to read and then go to sleep. Good night," Lennon said.

"Good night, Lennon," Mel responded.

***

The next morning, the sun illuminated the ranch with the most beautiful hot pink glow. Mel was in the kitchen brewing coffee while Lennon prepared a bowl of cereal. Mojo ate his breakfast and then went to beg for cereal. After breakfast, they walked to the truck where Slick was waiting.

"Mornin', y'all," Slick greeted.

"Mornin', Slick," Lennon responded.

"Good luck today. The truck and trailer are ready for departure. I loaded the hay net with alfalfa for the horse to eat on the road. I'm sure he'll be hungry," Slick said.

"Thank you much, Slick," Mel said as they pulled out.

"I still can't believe we're going back to San Bernardino. Does anyone over there take care of their animals?" Lennon asked.

"Yes, Lennon. Listen, animal cruelty happens everywhere. Being educated on what qualifies as animal abuse and being brave enough to report a person's questionable activity is super important as members of a community. If something doesn't feel right, that's your instinct telling you something. Trust it. It's most certainly right. Animals can't defend themselves, so we must do it for them. That applies to people too. We must do the right thing if we want to live in a kinder world. Take this woman, Lois, for example. She saw a bad situation and stepped in to help place the animals in good homes rather than turning a blind eye," Mel said.

"Yeah, but if the bad people left, why does Lois need to guard the horse?" Lennon asked.

"Well, she wants to make sure nothing does happen to him. She wants to meet us and make sure no one else comes onto the property and takes the horse. She really cares for him," Mel answered.

When they pulled up, a lady stood outside, waving them down. She wore an oversized white tee-shirt, jeans, and giant pink sunglasses. "You must be Mel?" she shouted. "I'm Lois. Been waiting for you."

"Is this the house?" Mel asked while pointing to a driveway with two massive concrete pillars at the entrance.

"Sure is. Not sure how you'll fit that big trailer in there, though," Lois said. "The horse is in the back."

After a few unsuccessful tries, it was clear that the trailer wouldn't fit. This meant that the only way this horse would get off the property was to walk himself out. Mel got out of the truck. Lennon held Mojo's leash and brought a halter.

"Follow me. I'll take you to him. Then we can figure out what to do since the trailer doesn't fit," Lois said.

The property was a junkyard. There were cars with missing wheels and broken windshields, a small motorboat, a toppled-over basketball hoop, fences, and metal scraps. In the far back corner was a small stall where a sad horse was lying. He didn't move when they approached his gate.

"This feels like Jude's house," Lennon stated.

"It has that same energy. So, Lennon, please stand outside his stall and hold Mojo's leash and the halter while I approach him.

Remember, we don't know him, and he doesn't know us, so it's important to be extra cautious," Mel said.

"Got it. I'll wait by the gate," Lennon responded.

Mel walked around the horse, inspecting his body. When he could see her, Mel got down on her knees. She looked at his hooves that were overgrown and his bum hoof that was facing the wrong direction. It was worse than the pictures portrayed. His back and hips had angry bedsores the size of softballs infected with blood and puss from lying in the dirt all day. His ribs were showing due to malnourishment. This horse was not in good condition and had been suffering for a long time. Mel sat on the ground and started to gently pat his face. He allowed her to be close. After a few minutes of sitting together, Mel looked into his eyes and said, "Listen, I am here to help you. I want to get you off this property and to a place where doctors can treat your wounds and help you heal. I'm here, promising you a better life, but I need something from you. I need you to walk yourself off this property. My trailer doesn't fit, and it's parked about 25 yards down the road. When you get there, we'll leave this place forever."

The horse moved his head back and forth. He was thinking about what he wanted to do.

"You do, however, have a choice. Come with me, and I promise you a better, happier life. Or stay, and I can have my vet come out today, and we can help you pass away peacefully into another world and take you out of this pain. Either way, I will not leave your side. You've been through so much. I know you deserve better. I want you to know you deserve better. You didn't do anything wrong in receiving this treatment. You are a good boy," Mel said.

The horse looked at Mel, thought for a few moments, and adjusted his back hooves under his body. He rocked back and forth a few times to gain momentum. He lifted the back part of his body first, brought his front hooves to their knees, and eventually got himself up. It looked painful and exhausting. His face was tense, his eyes were wide open, and his nostrils flared widely. He shook the dust off his body and made eye contact with Mel.

"Good boy. I'll walk over to the gate and get a halter and lead rope. I am going to be putting this around your head. Then together, we will walk out of here," Mel said. "Hey, Lennon, can you hand me the halter, please?"

Lennon handed Mel the halter, and Mel put the halter around his head without a fight.

Because his body suffered from muscle deterioration and fatigue, he had to think about each step and what motion was the least painful. He took five steps, stopped, looked around, and sighed. A positive sign, releasing tension. He took another two steps and then refused to walk further.

"Lennon, can you and Mojo run to the truck and grab the bag of cut-up watermelon and a water bucket?" Mel asked.

"Back in a jiffy," Lennon said and flew off with Mojo.

"Lennon and Mojo just ran to the trailer to get you some treats and water. We'll take our time getting there, but I need you to see the trailer. I want you to see where you are going. I want you to know that each small step we take together adds up, and soon, you will be off this property," Mel said.

Lennon came back and handed the bag to Mel. Mel began feeding him pieces. He loved it.

"Give me the water bucket. I'll fill it up," Lois said and walked to the hose located on the side of the house.

Lennon held Mojo's leash, and they stood by Mel and the horse. Five minutes passed, and the horse swayed back to take a step forward. They had taken seven steps and then rested. Lois held the water bucket up so he could drink. Mel gave him more watermelon. Lennon talked to the horse. "You can do this. I promise you can do this."

They managed to take a few more steps. This time, the horse stopped near a bamboo tree.

"Wait a minute. I can give him some bamboo leaves. I remember reading in one of my horse books that bamboo is good for them," Lennon said and tore the leaves off the tree, handing them to Mel.

"Here you go, handsome," Mel said while feeding the horse.

The horse showed great interest in the bamboo and waited for a second helping before taking the next round of steps.

It took two hours to get the horse to walk 25 yards from the stall to the trailer. By the time he arrived at the ramp, he was exhausted. He tried to lift his injured hoof onto the ramp but was having difficulty lifting and stabilizing. He was also having a hard time putting weight on the other hoof to take a step up. Mel tried luring him with treats filled with molasses, but nothing worked.

At this point, some neighbors gathered around to see the commotion. Lois explained the situation. They asked how they could help, and Mel devised a plan. She placed three men on one side of the horse and three on the other. She handed them a long rope wrapped around the horse's hind end, giving him support and the push he needed. Next, Mel instructed both sides to pull forward on the count of three. It worked. Everyone cheered and hugged when the horse got into the trailer.

Mel secured the halter and whispered, "I promised you a second chance, and I will not let you down." Mel thanked Lois for keeping a watchful and caring eye on him and drove off.

The hospital was two hours away. The vet techs prepared a stall, and their doctor was on call, ready to see him. The receptionist phoned Mel's cell to check in on their arrival and asked for the horse's name. Mel, without delay, said, "Chance." Lennon shouted from the back seat, "Avocado." And so, his name became Chance Avocado.

"Well, that's a new one," Greer, the front desk receptionist said and hung up the phone.

"How did you get avocado, Lennon?" Mel asked.

"Remember when you told me avocados were symbols of love? Well, what we're doing is a symbol of love," Lennon answered.

'I can't believe you remembered that!" Mel was shocked by Lennon's response.

"Why Chance?" asked Lennon.

"I promised him a second chance if he walked off this property. And we're going to give him everything he needs. He wants a new beginning, and we'll honor that," Mel said.

"Cool." Lennon watched Chance Avocado the entire ride as Slick set up the camera inside the trailer. There was space in the trailer for him to lay down, but he stood the whole ride and didn't eat any hay.

When they arrived, a team greeted them. Mel opened the trailer doors, put down the ramp, and began leading him off the trailer. But Chance Avocado was not moving. One of the vet techs got in and tried as well. Finally, he backed himself out, and when all four hooves landed on the ground, he looked at the team and didn't know what to make of the situation.

"I know this is a lot. Your day has been intense emotionally and physically. But, you have a few more steps to go, and you can sleep all night. There is bedding, hay, and water waiting for you," Mel said.

Chance Avocado allowed Mel to lead him to his stall, and right before he entered, his hind legs started to buckle and give out from under him so quickly that the vet techs came over to support and push him. In the stall, he put his front knees down and let his back collapse. He faced the wall away from the door and slept.

While Mel was signing the intake forms, Lennon stood on a bale of hay, peeking in, and talking to him about anything that came to her mind. "This is a horse hospital. You are safe here, Chance Avocado. We couldn't bring you back to Moonlight Mile Ranch because you need to see the doctors first. There are lemon and avocado fields that surround this place. Next time we come, I'll bring you an avocado so you can see what you are named after. You can't eat it, though, as it will make you sick. Avocados are one of my favorite fruits,"

Mel sat down on the bale of hay near Lennon. The vet came over and sat next to her. "What a day. I can't believe we are finally here," Mel said.

"I'm sure," Dr. Keller said.

"So, what do you think? Does he have a chance?" Mel asked.

"Chance Avocado didn't come all this way to not keep going. We're going to treat him, and we're going to help him. This will take time and patience on your end. But one day, he'll leave this hospital and head back to your ranch. The boys back home will be thrilled. You guys did good work. Now, if you excuse me, we'll begin running bloodwork and tests on him to make sure we can put him on pain killers," Dr. Keller said.

"Thank you. I called my farrier and set up an appointment. He'll be here in two days. Wanted Chance to have some time to decompress before we start addressing his hooves," Mel said.

"Great thinking. Our team will be here," Dr. Keller said.

The sun was starting to set, and Mel knew it was time to leave. Everyone was exhausted. She went into the stall to say goodnight to Chance. "I'm sorry you had to endure all that pain to end up here. But roads lead to places. And we travel down them for a reason. I am grateful your road led to my family. The people here are going to help you. We will be back tomorrow. Get some rest, my sweet boy," and she kissed him on the head.

***

The following day, Mel dropped Lennon off at school and drove to the hospital. As Mel and Mojo walked down the barn hall, Mel was nervous about what she'd see in stall seven. Was Chance going to be standing, lying down, alive? So many thoughts ran through her head. And when they arrived, Chance was lying down on a massive pile of soft shavings, sleeping.

"Hey, Mel. I wanted to let you know that I put down extra shavings this morning to soften Chance's bed after cleaning his stall. I want him to be extra comfortable here," Trevor said. Trevor was the farm hand at the hospital, responsible for cleaning stalls and feeding the horses. Because he was in charge of the feedings, all the horses loved seeing him and let out loud neighs to get his attention.

"Thanks, man. I think Chance appreciates your kindness. How was he this morning?" Mel asked.

"He stood up for breakfast and ate out of the feeder, but not for long. So, I put some hay on the ground so he can eat laying down," Trevor said.

"Smart thinking," Mel responded.

Dr. Keller came over. "Morning, Mel. His body is healthy. We started him on painkillers. He is underweight, as we can see. But that we'll correct over time and with a proper meal plan. Your farrier will be here tomorrow, yeah?"

"Correct, at 10 a.m.," Mel responded.

"Perfect. See you then," Dr. Keller said and walked to the next stall to treat a different horse.

Mel and Mojo entered stall seven and sat down on the ground next to Chance. Mojo sniffed and licked Chance's face and then settled into the side of Mel's leg. Mel sat, petting Chance's face, brushing his fur and braiding his mane to keep him cool. Chance needed to rest. They sat together until it was time to pick Lennon up at school.

The next morning was the same routine. Lennon went to school while Mel and Mojo drove to the hospital to meet Brett, the farrier. As the two walked down the barn hall, Mel was nervous and wondered how she would find Chance. Mel was relieved when she saw him standing up, eating breakfast. Trevor came over. "Chance has been standing all morning,"

"Incredible," Mel said.

Brett arrived at the same time Dr. Keller and the team ended their morning rounds. After introductions, Dr. Keller, Brett, and Mel went into Chance's stall to look at his hoofs and examined the x-rays. Their goal was to go as short as possible on the bum hoof without cutting into soft tissue and trim the rest down to a healthy length.

Brett returned to his truck and took out nippers, a forged knife, a stand, and an electric file. Once he set the space up, he took a moment alone with Chance. He put the halter around Chance's head and stood there with him. Brett wanted Chance to trust him and his energy.

Dr. Keller came over to sedate Chance, and two vet techs monitored his vitals. Mel held the halter and softly reassured him that everything was going to be okay.

Brett started with the bum hoof. First, he used the nippers to cut and cut and cut away the overgrown and infected hoof. Next, he used the knife and file to flatten any sharp or uneven edges. By the time he was done, Brett had taken off about two inches of hoof.

Brett then worked on Chance's hind hoofs, removing three inches of the hoof on each foot. When Brett moved to the front right hoof, Chance refused to lift it. Sedated and on painkillers, it was still too much of an ask. Chance was not comfortable putting weight on the bum hoof. Dr. Keller walked Chance down the hall and into a stall with a large animal lift. They placed a harness around his body, and Dr. Keller, Mel, and the two techs began hoisting Chance off the ground. This allowed Brett to work without Chance putting weight on his legs.

Three and a half hours later, Chance's hooves were trimmed enough to provide some relief. Chance walked back into his stall to rest for the night.

A few weeks later, Mel, Lennon, and Mojo drove to the hospital to visit Chance. Lennon hopped out of the truck and walked directly to the avocado field where she picked one up off the ground to bring to Chance. "I told him I'd bring him an avocado, and that is just what I am doing." Lennon showed Mel a giant ripe avocado.

Together, they walked down the barn hall, and Mel was less nervous about what she would find in stall seven. Chance was getting stronger every day, and, over time, the doctors recorded significant improvements, such as weight gain and longer periods of standing. When they arrived, Lennon shouted, "Where is Chance Avocado? He isn't in his stall,"

"What do you mean he isn't in his stall?" Mel asked and rushed to look at the stall herself. Chance wasn't there.

Mel walked over to one of the vet techs and asked, "Any idea where Chance went?"

"We walked him to the turn-out for some exercise," the vet tech said.

"He walked to the turn-out for exercise?" Mel replied.

"New orders. Daily exercise. Go take a look," she pointed towards the exit on the other side of the barn.

The three of them swiftly walked to the turn-out, and there he was, standing in a round pen, looking at them, smiling almost. His face was soft, appreciative of fresh air and the sun hitting his back. He nickered with delight to see them.

"Chance Avocado, look, an avocado. I got this one from the field over there. I wanted to show you the fruit you are named after," Lennon said.

Dr. Keller came over. "How great is this."

"Without words. Truly without words," Mel said and hugged Dr. Keller.

"Everyone here is just as excited as you are. So, listen, Chance is having some trouble eating his hay. He needs a float. I want that done as soon as possible," Dr. Keller said.

"What's a float?" Lennon asked.

"A float is a dental examination. And Chance here has three hook teeth that need to be filed down. They're causing head tension and pain while eating," Dr. Keller responded.

"What is a hook tooth?" Lennon asked.

"Think of it like a tiger tooth. Sharp. Horses don't need sharp teeth. They eat hay, not meat. Flat teeth are best for grinding down the hay," Dr. Keller said

"Chance is an herbivore. Of course. I should have known," Lennon said.

"I'll confirm a date and time with Greer, and we can get that done this week," Mel said.

"Excellent. Lennon, could you take the halter and lead Chance back to his stall? He's been out here for over an hour, and lunch will be served soon," Dr. Keller asked.

"Umm, yes." Lennon walked Chance back to his stall where he stood waiting for Trevor to come by with a bucket of grain and hay. After lunch, they drove home and hung out with their horses.

That night, Slick, June, Mel, Lennon, and Mojo made a small bonfire to honor the full moon. The more June and Lennon learned about regenerative farming, the more they paid attention to the moon cycles. Moon cycles are the best time to harvest, plant, or flip soil.

"Now that we are all here, what's happening with Chance?" Slick asked.

"Doing better," Mel said.

"His progress is, well, like a caterpillar . Very, very, very slow. Even slower than what you think, but progressing," Lennon said.

"Well, that was a brilliant explanation, Lennon," June replied.

"Yes, it was." Mel smiled.

"Now that we farm, I've been learning about worms," Lennon said.

"You know the coolest part about being a caterpillar? It's when they enter the chrysalis stage. Then, the caterpillar's body dies and transforms into a beautiful butterfly. It is one of the most magnificent transformations in nature," Mel said.

"I see that the full moon makes you all philosophical, and I can appreciate that. Is Chance going to come live here at the ranch?" Slick asked.

"One day. When? I am not sure. He has been in the hospital for over a month. We should start building a small pasture for him near the boys, so he has a herd but, at the same time, is well protected. We need to keep him safe. You very well know that Hickory can kick and destroy a fence, and Ollie has the special skill of unlocking chain fences. So we really need to secure his area," Mel said.

"I'll get on it tomorrow," Slick said.

The fire had died out, but in the darkness of Malibu, the moon shone brightly, and it seemed as if every constellation in the sky was visible. Mel tucked Lennon in and retired to the couch with Mojo to have tea before she fell asleep too.

That week, Chance had his teeth floated and felt more relief when eating. Dr. Keller was quite pleased with the results and could approximate his age to be 13 years old. Chance stayed in the turn-out longer and longer each day. He was slowly putting on more weight, and when Brett returned to trim his hooves, he took less and less off and needed less sedation. He was starting to look and stand like a horse.

One Saturday, Mel, Lennon, and Mojo visited Chance, and when they arrived at stall seven, there was a big yellow sticker that read, "CLEARED TO GO HOME."

Confused, Mel and Lennon walked to the doctor's office, and there was Dr. Keller, the two vet techs, Trevor and Greer, smiling. "We wanted this to be a surprise. Chance is healthy and ready to go back to Moonlight Mile Ranch. Moreover, there is nothing we are doing here that you couldn't do at your ranch. Except give him more love," Dr. Keller said.

"Chance has been here for over two months. I've come every day to visit him. I have seen so many horses come and go. I often wondered when, if, it would be his turn. So while I'm excited, I'm insanely nervous too. Chance has been supported by the most wonderful team here," Mel said, holding on to Lennon and Mojo.

"You, Lennon, and Mojo are part of his team. Better yet, you are his family. And we will always support Chance. If anything comes up, your ranch is only thirty minutes away. We will come over," Dr. Keller said. "And listen, I'm not going to tell you how to feel, but as his doctor, I wouldn't release him if I had an inkling of doubt. Chance is ready to go home. Be confident and trust these orders. I know how you spoil your boys and it's time to spoil him too."

Mel took a deep breath and hugged Dr. Keller and the entire team.

"Like a caterpillar," Lennon said. One of the vet techs looked a little confused about Lennon's comment, but the moment was so grand that no one paid attention or felt the need to explain Lennon's analogy to the confused vet tech.

"My big caterpillar, you did it. You are coming home with us," Lennon said. Chance looked at Lennon and put his head down so she could kiss his nose. Chance was extra gentle towards Lennon and Mojo.

"Chance, you have clearance to leave the hospital. I didn't anticipate how powerful those words were. Lennon is right. You are the biggest caterpillar there ever was, and you are transforming into the most beautiful butterfly. You inspire me, Chance. Your story will inspire others. We'll be back tomorrow to get you," Mel said.

When they got home, Mel told Slick the news. Chance's pasture was complete and ready for his arrival. Slick constructed a small area with layers of soft dirt for him to rest comfortably. The fencing was an old wood that created horse rails with welded wire to add protection. There were two locks so no horse, not Hickory or Ollie, could break down or break into Chance's pasture. His food and water bins were on the ground, so he had easy access if he wanted to eat lying down. A beautiful pepper tree extended into his pasture, creating a natural shade spot.

The following day, Mel, Lennon, and Mojo arrived at the hospital. They parked as close to his stall as possible, so he didn't have to walk far. Mel checked in with the doctors, and the entire staff that treated him came over to say goodbye, which was unusual. It was evident that everyone there loved him and was rooting for his recovery. Trevor gave him a special goodbye as he spent the most time in the stall with him. Mel invited the team to the ranch for lunch whenever they needed a day off to relax and enjoy being in nature. Dr. Keller reminded Mel to call if anything comes up. Mel thanked the staff. Lennon brought in lemons from the field and handed one to Dr. Keller, Trevor, the two vet techs, and Greer from the front office. "Thank you. Here is a lemon to make lemonade," Lennon said to them.

Chance Avocado walked out of the stall with confidence. And though he was limping, he made no stops on the way to the trailer. When he arrived at the ramp, he looked down and up and walked carefully into the trailer. While Mel secured him, he noshed on hay.

"Well, this trailer ride is very different than the last one we had with him," Mel said.

"Sure is," Lennon commented.

As they drove out of the hospital parking lot, *Lovely* Day by Bill Withers was playing. Mel took a deep breath in and let all the air go. She rolled down her windows, put on her cowboy hat, and drove them all home.

When they arrived, Slick and June were at the pasture. Mel walked Chance out of the trailer. He paused, looked around, and let out a loud neigh. He knew he was home. He knew he did it. As he reached his pasture, the boys came to meet the new guy. Peanut extended his neck as far as he could to touch noses with Chance. Hickory did kick, which was expected, and Ollie made his donkey noises of excitement that sounded like a busted horn. Chance kept his distance. This was his first time having horse friends. He wasn't sure what to make of it.

Weeks later, the boys were bonding through the fence. Mel would put hay down, and they would all eat close to one another. Peanut and Chance would smell each other, and Ollie would watch over Chance when he took long afternoon naps. Whenever Brett came to trim Chance, Ollie paced with concern. Ollie was reassured that Chance was okay with treats and extra love. Chance had good and bad days, but the bad days were getting fewer. He was able to walk around the property slowly as part of his rehabilitation. His bedsores were getting smaller but not entirely gone. He was eating well and gained forty pounds. Dr. Keller came out several times for x-rays of his hoof and overall health checks and was pleased with the progress. Slick gave Chance a morning bowl of grain and supplements. June would bring Chance carrots from the garden. Mel, Lennon, and Mojo would sit in his pasture and read books to him. The other horses pushed their bodies against the fence to hear the stories. It was an excellent way to spend time together without asking Chance to do much of anything. There was beauty in rest, and rest allowed his body to recover. Chance showed Mel the intensity of healing and how the path to recovery isn't always a straight line. Although setbacks occur and are part of life, that doesn't mean giving up hope.

Mel kept her word and delivered Chance a life filled with love, family, and friendship. She helped Chance restore his faith in humans. Chance was no longer in servitude, a rare thing for a horse. All Chance had to do was be himself, and that was enough.

Word got out around town about this horse, and people reached out to Mel as they wanted to meet him. And so, Mel shared his story with those interested. Chance connected with people of all ages and backgrounds. He had such grounding energy. One visitor was so moved that she wrote a poem about him and submitted it to the local Malibu newspaper.

Then one day, the Dodo reached out to Mel as they wanted to feature Chance's story on their social media platforms. Mel had some hesitation at first as the internet welcomes both positive and negative energy in a way no one can control. But, after much thought and talking to Chance, Mel decided that his story was important. Within a few days of his video being aired, it received over 5.5 million views, and the comments, and there were thousands, were so kind. Strangers worldwide were so grateful that this deserving horse got a second chance. What Mel noticed was that people related to Chance Avocado's story. Those that came to meet him saw themselves in his struggle and identified with learning how to trust again, living with a physical disability, and overcoming trauma. Chance Avocado, that sad horse abandoned in a backyard, went on to touch the lives of millions. But to Chance, he was happiest knowing he found himself a family with people, dogs, and horses that loved and cared deeply for him.

And while this story ends, their journey is just beginning.

NOTES FROM THE AUTHOR

This book shares the stories of some animals our family rescued at Moonlight Mile Ranch. We aspire to create a shift in thinking, allowing more space in your heart to live in harmony with the world. When we see ourselves as one and not as the superior species, we treat our surroundings with respect. I hope these brave animals who have gone through despair to discover love and a new life demonstrate that kindness and love are not only possible but critical to our connections.

Impactful change happens when we examine our daily choices. Through individual action, the world is ours to make better. May this book inspire you to advocate for those who don't have a voice, empathize with the less fortunate, and help those in need.

About the Author

Mel Sobolewski has been rescuing, evacuating, and rehabilitating animals since the Woolsey Fire in Malibu, California, in 2018. Each animal rescue was so impactful that, over time, she left her corporate job and turned this into a way of life.

Mel is inspired by music, poetry, and books. Many of the animals and characters in this book are based on cultural icons. Her family's love of music can often times lead to impromptu living room dance parties with Lennon, Mojo, and their friends. While Mojo isn't too pleased with everyone jumping around, he does find his way into Mel's arms and prefers to be carried while everyone dances around him. Mojo is a sixty-pound labradoodle. At the ranch, Hickory, Mel's first rescue horse, prefers Taylor Swift. Any other artist will cause him to buck wildly in his pasture. Mel, Lennon, and Mojo can also be seen reading to the horses. Their favorite book is *The Boy, the Mole, the Fox and the Horse* by Charles Mackesy. There is nothing more soulful than reading time with the animals at Moonlight Mile Ranch.

The two motivating reasons why Mel wrote this book was to share the stories of these animals and show that animals are more like us than we assume them to be, in terms of trust, friendship, patience, and love. The other reason was to engage with kids as Mel is inspired by a kid's mind, heart, curiosity, quest for truth, adventure, and joy.

Mel Sobolewski grew up in Long Island, New York, graduated from the University of Wisconsin-Madison. She has been invited to lobby animal welfare laws on a state and federal level and was part of the team responsible for passing the fur ban in California, a significant bill as California was the first state to ban the sale of fur. Mel's rescues have been featured on news networks nationwide, morning radio-shows, magazines and on impactful social media handles.

Mel resides in Los Angeles, California, with her dog Mojo, her two cats, Leo and Fifi, and her daughter, Lennon.

To learn more about Moonlight Mile Ranch, please visit www.moonlightmileranch.com

www.ingramcontent.com/pod-product-compliance
Lightning Source LLC
Chambersburg PA
CBHW071312150726
47997CB00002B/459